An introduction to therapeutic communities

Department of Social and Administrative Studies,
Barnett House,
Wellington Square,
Oxford.

KENNARD, David & ROBERTS, Jeff   HP 54

Introduction to Therapeutic
Communities, An.

The International Library of
Group Psychotherapy and Group Process

Therapeutic Communities Section

Section Editors

R. D. Hinshelwood
Consultant Psychotherapist
St Bernard's Hospital, Southall, Middlesex

Nick Manning
Lecturer in Social Policy and Administration
University of Kent

An introduction to therapeutic communities

David Kennard

with a joint contribution by
Jeff Roberts

Routledge & Kegan Paul
London, Boston, Melbourne and Henley

First published in 1983
by Routledge & Kegan Paul plc
39 Store Street, London WC1E 7DD
9 Park Street, Boston, Mass. 02108, USA,
464 St. Kilda Road, Melbourne,
Victoria 3004 Australia, and
Broadway House, Newtown Road,
Henley-on-Thames, Oxon RG9 1EN
Printed in Great Britain by
The Thetford Press Ltd., Thetford, Norfolk
© David Kennard 1983
Chapter 10 © David Kennard and Jeff Roberts 1983

Library of Congress Cataloging in Publication Data

Kennard, David.

An introduction to therapeutic communities.
(The International library of group psychotherapy
and group process; therapeutic communities section)
Bibliography: p.
Includes index.
1. Therapeutic community. I. Roberts, Jeff.
II. Title. III. Series: International library of group
psychotherapy and group process.   [DNLM: 1. Therapeutic
community. WM 440 K34i]
RC489.T67K45   1983   362.2   83-8697

ISBN 0-7100-9577-5

Contents

Preface

Something which I am tempted to call the 'therapeutic community impulse' flows through many forms of institutional care,
or rather in the people who create them. I mean institution
in the sense of any place where people live together (or come
together daily) because they can no longer manage to live in
their usual family or social environment or are no longer
wanted there. These include special schools, psychiatric
hospitals, prisons, hostels, day centres. The impulse is
difficult to define. It expresses itself in a number of
attitudes: liberalism, egalitarianism, psychological minded-
ness, toleration of the expression of conflicting ideas, and
a kind of shirt-sleeves informality about the business of
helping people. It is an impulse to focus on the quality of
relationships and communication between people, on the way
they naturally set about dealing with one another, as the
essential working material of treatment. This impulse contrasts with others, for example the impulse to make people as
uniform and easy to manage as possible, which is found in
many institutions as well as in more repressive societies.
Or the impulse to look after people in a protective but controlling way which is characteristic of many good hospitals.

I am inclined to believe that these impulses are aspects
of human nature and are thus all present, to a greater or
lesser extent, in the ways people have tried to help one
another at different times and in different places. The
therapeutic community impulse has appeared more or less
strongly in different specialities, in different countries,
and in different periods of their history.

Sometimes it has been accompanied by conscientious
thoughtfulness and produced long-lived and well-researched
communities. At other times by enthusiastic but naive

dogmatism, producing short-lived or Messianic communities.
At various times it has been linked to different theories of
interpersonal relations.   The Christian belief that love
will eventually elicit the good in even the worst offender
guided many early leaders of therapeutic communities.   Later
pioneers were more likely to be guided by Freud's theories of
unconscious forces pushing people into repetitions of unhappy
relationships, for which the cure was understanding rather
than love alone.   More recently many therapeutic communities
have been influenced by those theories broadly labelled as
'humanistic-existential', which emphasise the responsibility
each of us has for deciding what kind of person we want to
be.

   In its various forms and with its changing travelling com-
panions, the therapeutic community impulse has continued to
express itself in a wide variety of caring establishments.
In this book I have tried to document some of the main forms
this expression has taken.

I have written this book primarily for students and trainees
in the helping professions who may spend some time in a therapeutic community or come across the idea and want to know
more about it.   It is also for those who have recently begun
to work in a helping community of one sort or another, or are
considering whether to do so.   A further aim of the book is
to introduce therapeutic communities to one another.   People
who work in one kind of community often know little of what
goes on in others, and I hope this book will help to correct
a few misconceptions and enable practitioners to feel more
informed about each other's approach.   Finally I hope it
will be useful to anyone who is interested to find out what
therapeutic communities are, how they came about, and the
ideas and skills relevant to them.

   There are two parts.   The first provides a detailed description of the way different kinds of therapeutic communities have evolved.   This begins with a chapter bringing
together the features they share in common - something I want
to emphasise, which is why it starts the book.   Chapters 2-6
then describe four kinds of community in terms of their history, ideas and practice.   Chapter 7 summarises the distinctive attributes of these four types and the range of ideas on
which any particular therapeutic community can draw.   Research findings have not been dealt with as a separate topic
but incorporated at relevant points.

The second part is addressed specifically to those readers
who are concerned about the experience and practicalities of
working in a therapeutic community. Chapter 8 presents an
imaginary 'first day' which will bring the material in Part I
to life for readers who have not actually been in a therapeutic community, and may help those who have to recognise some
of the responses of a newcomer. Chapter 9 offers some practical guidelines for beginners and Chapter 10 discusses questions related to the needs and resources for training in
therapeutic community work. This chapter was written jointly with Jeff Roberts, a colleague and collaborator on many
training ventures. Being able to challenge and question
each other's ideas as we prepared this chapter helped us
avoid the pitfall of assuming one's own personal opinion to
be the best source of wisdom.

At the end of the book there is an information section for
those who want to extend their acquaintance with therapeutic
communities. It provides information about communities,
relevant associations and training organisations in many
countries. Jeff Roberts gathered and compiled the information for Great Britain and I did this for the other countries.

In writing an introductory book covering different types of
therapeutic communities, there is a risk - a likelihood -
that my own experience and point of view have influenced the
way things are presented. While I have tried to give an
accurate picture of each approach inevitably there is personal judgment, not least about what to include and what to
leave out. It may help the reader to be aware of the framework within which the book was put together, if I say what my
own interests and experience have been. My interest in
therapeutic communities goes back about fifteen years. The
mid-1960s was the heyday of anti-psychiatry, and as a recent
psychology graduate I was drawn to the writings of Ronald
Laing and other existential psychotherapists. I visited
Kingsley Hall two or three times and became interested in
trying to understand mental illness. This led to an interest in mental hospitals and what went on inside them. I
worked briefly as a psychiatric nursing assistant and then
decided to take a job as a probationer clinical psychologist.
While training I became interested in social and interpersonal aspects of psychiatry and found a natural liking for
working in groups. A visit to the Henderson hospital
impressed me, and on qualifying in 1970 I moved to Littlemore
hospital in Oxford, where I worked until 1982. There I was
able to become involved in two different therapeutic communi-

ties. One was a psychiatric admission unit, the other was a
new unit for drug abusers which evolved into a self-help
therapeutic community partly staffed by former drug addicts.
This side-by-side experience prompted several attempts to
conceptualise the differences between the two which, looking
back, were the beginnings of this book. In addition I
became increasingly involved in the activities of the Association of Therapeutic Communities, and through this visited
many other communities.

Two experiences have had a particular influence on my
approach to writing this book. Research projects which I
carried out in the above two communities in collaboration
with Robert Clemmey and Steve Wilson taught me a lot about
ordering information, thinking through conceptual problems,
and trying to stay within the evidence when making statements. Although this is not a book about research, the
discipline of writing it has been similar. The other experience has been my training as a group analyst. Being a
patient in an analytic group and participating in a group-
analytic climate of supervision and discussion has created a
perspective which links at a deep level the individual's experience with the way people feel and act in groups and communities. This is a perspective which makes therapeutic
communities - and other institutions - fascinating places to
work in and think about.

Writing this book has taken many evenings and weekends
over nearly three years. During this time my wife and I had
our first son who discovered quite early on that one of the
more intriguing objects in the house was the box with buttons
on it that his father was endlessly tapping. To my fellow
typist Joseph and to Claire, who always believed I could
write this book when I often doubted it myself, I dedicate
the book.

Oxford
October 1982

Acknowledgments

The following people made valuable comments on various parts
of the book: Liz Burrows, Brian Donellan, George Dunne,
Joanne Evans, Heinz Fischer, Bob Hinshelwood, Margaret
Howarth, Carolyn Lawson, Liz Smith, Caroline Trimnell and
Sue Vogt.

I am grateful to the staff and residents of the following
therapeutic communities for allowing me to visit and discus-
sing with me their views and impressions: Arbours Crisis
Centre, Ascot Farm, Church Lane Community, Cotswold Community,
Henderson Hospital, Ingrebourne Centre, Rutland House,
St Charles House.

In particular I am grateful to my colleagues in the
Phoenix Unit and Ley Community. The constant interplay of
feelings and ideas in these communities has been the testing
ground against which the ideas for this book have gradually
taken shape. To Peter Agulnik, John McCabe and Bertram
Mandelbrote I feel a special debt for the stimulation of
their ideas and working approach.

Many friends and colleagues in the Association of Therapeutic Communities have provided inspiration in our formal
and informal get-togethers, and to them I should like to
express my gratitude.

Tom Main kindly gave permission to quote at length from
his lecture, The Concept of the Therapeutic Community: Variations and Vicissitudes, which appeared in 'Group Analysis' as
a supplement to vol. 10 (2), 1977.

Finally I should like to thank Verlaine Bowden, who typed
and retyped the many drafts through which the book has passed
with interest and good humour.
xi

Part I

Therapeutic communities within and beyond psychiatry

Part 1

Chapter 1
Different origins - common attributes

People use the phrase 'a therapeutic community' to describe
different sorts of ventures. Since no one has a copyright on
it, and there is no generally agreed system for classifying
such communities, some confusion cannot be avoided. That is
not necessarily a bad thing. Limiting the term to one type
of community might do more harm than good, inhibiting further
development, or 'outlawing' certain types of community which
might be just as therapeutic as those within the definition.
Yet despite their different origins and circumstances, organisations which are known as therapeutic communities do appear
to have a number of important attributes in common. What I
shall try to do in this chapter is indicate the different ways
in which the term has been used, and then describe those
features which I believe most of these ventures have in
common.

DIFFERENT ORIGINS

How have the different uses of the term come about?   The
first difference is that it can be used in a general or specific way. In a 'general' way, any hospital, correctional or
educational institution that is trying to improve the lot of
its inmates by offering them opportunities for productive,
responsible work, for developing their interests and talents,
and above all opportunities for participating in the day-to-
day running of the institution, may call itself a therapeutic
community. The term is often used in this way when the place
in question was until recently considered to be decidedly un-
therapeutic. It indicates the wish of a particular institution to dissociate itself from its sorry or sordid past.
Mental hospitals may call themselves therapeutic communities
to indicate the new leaf they have turned over in bringing

patients normal, decent living conditions, and creating a more
humane, stimulating atmosphere. In Great Britain the need to
use the term in this way has receded as mental hospitals have
generally become more humane and liberal places in which to
live, although there is still some way to go. In countries
where the mentally ill are still locked up in regimented,
overcrowded, insanitary conditions, this meaning of 'therapeutic community' can still be a rousing banner to march
under. In order to distinguish this meaning from the more
specific one, it has been called the 'therapeutic community
approach'. (1)

Using the term in a 'specific' way, therapeutic community
refers to a particular set of principles and methods used to
help people with particular kinds of problems or disorders.
This brings us to a second source of confusion. By what
appears to be historical coincidence the same term was introduced independently in England and the United States, twelve
years apart but none the less as far as one can tell quite
independently. In England, psychiatrist and psychoanalyst
Tom Main first wrote about therapeutic communities in 1946.
At that time he was using the term mainly in the general
sense described above, but over the decade that followed
there emerged a distinctive therapeutic community method,
largely associated with the work of Maxwell Jones at the
Henderson Hospital. Clark has called this 'therapeutic community proper', to distinguish it from the general
'approach'. (2) It had as its hallmark the democratic
sharing of power by all members of the community - staff and
patients alike - in decisions which affected not only the
running of the community but also the treatment of the
patients. Patients became auxiliary therapists and official
hierarchies were reduced as far as possible. More will be
said about this kind of therapeutic community later. At
this point enough has been said to contrast it with what
emerged, 6,000 miles away in California, in 1958.

A man named Charles Dederich, an ex-alcoholic who had
become an ardent member of Alcoholics Anonymous but was dissatisfied with some of its limitations, founded an organisation called Synanon where ex-alcoholics and ex-drug addicts
could live together and help one another to stay 'clean' i.e.
drug-free. The basic principle was a 'no-holds-barred'
honest confrontation about anything and everything. Emotion-
Emotional defences or 'copouts' were demolished in verbally
aggressive encounter groups known as the 'Synanon Game'.
The atmosphere was one of righteous, some might say religious,
zeal. Apart from this difference of general tone from the

English communities, there were two other major differences.
One was that Synanon and many of the communities that followed
in its footsteps were run by non-professionals, run in fact by
ex-addicts for ex-addicts.   Professionals such as psychiatrists and psychologists were distrusted or seen as having
little to offer.   The second difference was the hierarchical
structure that Synanon developed.   Ironically, while doctors
and nurses in English therapeutic communities were busy dis-
mantling some, if not all of their authority, sharing decisions with patients and striving towards greater informality
and equality, ex-addicts in Synanon and elsewhere were busy
creating a steeply graded staff and resident hierarchy where
decisions were made at the top and obeyed at the bottom, and
failure at either end meant confrontation in the encounter
group that night.   And all in the name of the therapeutic
community!

More will be said later about the philosophies and practice
of these two types of therapeutic community, but at this point
it seems that we really should ask the question, do they have
anything in common other than the name, and the broad aim of
helping people?   I think the answer to this is undoubtedly
yes - most of the ingredients are the same, only organised in
a different way - but this is not the view taken by all therapeutic community workers.   In fact people who work in one or
other of these two types of therapeutic community often know
very little about the other type.   Listen to one of the
speakers at the Second World Conference of Therapeutic Communities, held in Canada in 1977: 'The entire therapeutic community movement of the world - now involving more than 2,000
facilities and perhaps 100,000 narcotics addicts - started
with one man, Charles Dederich.' (3)   Not true.   Now listen
to this comment by one of the pioneers of therapeutic communities in England, writing of Synanon and its offshoots:

> They are communities and they are therapeutic, but they do
> not pretend to be therapeutic communities as described by
> Maxwell Jones.   They have an authoritarian structure, with
> punishments and degredations, harsher than could be tolera-
> ted in any organisation run by doctors and nurses. (4)

This is factually correct, but implies that Maxwell Jones, the
best-known pioneer of the English egalitarian model of a therapeutic community, somehow has a copyright on the term.   But
as I suggested at the beginning of this chapter, no one has
this.

Indeed others have used it who are followers of neither

Jones nor Dederich.   They too have sought to harness the
energies present in a small, close community, usually one that
shares a communal household, for the express purpose of helping some or all of its members to overcome or cope with their
personal inadequacies or distress.   Some of these have been
inspired by the ideas and work of the Christian philosopher
and educationalist Rudolf Steiner.   Others, like the network
of Richmond Fellowship half-way houses, emerged from a more
general concept of Christian fellowship.   And there are those
which were created in the wake of the anti-psychiatry movement
of the 1960s, associated with the writings of Ronald Laing and
David Cooper.

To summarise so far, there are four broad but distinct ways
in which the term therapeutic community is used, four main
kinds of venture to which it refers.   They are:

1 The transformation of large, asylum-type institutions,
usually containers for the chronically mentally ill, into
more active, humane, caring institutions where the human
rights and dignity of the inmates are recognised and respected.   Such a change usually goes hand in hand with
changes in social awareness and attitudes in the wider environment.   The organisation, if it is a hospital, is
still run by the doctors and nurses, whose task changes
from being custodians to creating an atmosphere in which
patients are trusted and encouraged to take responsibility
and initiative.

2 The development of small, cohesive communities where
therapeutic decisions and functions are shared by the
whole community, and where the status differences between
staff and resident are greatly reduced though not abandoned.   In the field of psychiatry such therapeutic communities are sometimes referred to as the Maxwell Jones or
democratic type.   In Great Britain the term 'therapeutic
community', when used to describe a small establishment in
the domain of mental health, social services or therapeutic
education usually refers to an enterprise of this type.
They most frequently deal with adolescents and young adults
suffering from problems of neurosis, personality disorder
or social maladjustment.

3 The development of small, cohesive communities in which
the staff and residents form a continuous hierarchy or
chain of command.   Staff are qualified for their work by
virtue of having been residents in such a community themselves.   The names Synanon, Daytop Village and Phoenix

House all refer to communities of this kind.   They are
also known as Concept Houses or concept-based therapeutic
communities.   Communities of this type are almost exclu-
sively concerned with the rehabilitation of alcoholics and
drug addicts, although attempts have been made to treat
other offenders in this way.

4 Dissatisfaction with conventional psychiatry and a concern with the spiritual, moral and social aspects of emotional distress have given rise to a number of communities
which offer an alternative to mental hospital treatment.
Some of these have been described as therapeutic communities.   They do not form a single type, but tend to share
certain features in common.   These include a strong commitment to a particular faith or philosophy of life, and an
emphasis on the equal status of all members.   There are
usually no labels of 'staff' or 'patient'.   It is also
characteristic of those communities which arose from the
anti-psychiatry movement of the 1960s that a member can
experience a psychotic breakdown without having it treated
as an illness.

COMMON ATTRIBUTES

Allowing for exceptions, it seems generally true that those
who have used the term therapeutic community have done so
with similar ideas and procedures in mind.   I have tried to
arrange these in an order roughly corresponding to how
visible or immediately apparent they are, starting with the
most apparent.

    The first is the informal and communal atmosphere which is
often the first thing to strike a visitor or newcomer to a
therapeutic community.   The atmosphere is homelike rather
than institutional, casual, perhaps untidy.   People are
dressed informally, no suits, no uniforms.   The visitor to a
hospital wonders, 'Who are the patients?' 'Who are the staff?'
What is definitely absent is the atmosphere of regimented
boredom common in large institutions, or the brisk white-
coated efficiency of the general hospital.   Neither is it a
hushed clinic.   Things are going on all around, not behind
closed doors.   Although informal, the atmosphere may not be
relaxed - argument, laughter, tears are all possible - all
out there in the open where anyone can see or even join in.
The newcomer is uneasily aware that some basic and expected
boundaries have ceased to operate.   Residents and staff are
not clearly and immediately distinguishable.   Events of a

rather private nature seem to be going on in public.   Of
course lack of boundaries may be more apparent than real.   On
further acquaintance the visitor may learn that the staff do
exert authority, or that the rather public airing of private
feelings involved a certain amount of display by a particular
individual.   Yet the atmosphere of informality is real
enough, and has much in common with the principle of 'Communalism' described by Rapaport in his book 'Community as Doctor'.
He named this as one of four general principles to which therapeutic communities adhere.

A second shared characteristic of all types of therapeutic
communities is the central place of group meetings in the
therapeutic programme.   These may take various forms but
there will be regular times, at least once a week, often
daily, when the whole community meets together, and other
times when members meet together in smaller groups.   The
purpose and sophistication of these meetings will vary considerably from one community to another, and the goals may not
always be fully stated or even recognised.   Regardless of the
type of community, however, the occurrence of these regular
meetings, especially of the whole community, helps to fulfil
the following functions:

1 To maximise the sharing of information; simply by
being there everyone is kept up to date, while anyone who
has information to impart to the rest of the community
(whether reporting events or giving opinions) has an effective means of doing so.   The community meeting is in this
sense a kind of living newspaper of the community.

2 To build a sense of cohesion, of togetherness within the
community; everyone can see and get to know something
about everyone else, can share in the hopes and fears expressed by other members, and in the day-to-day problems
and achievements of the community.

3 To make open and public the process of decision-making;
in some communities residents and staff decide jointly what
to do about a particular matter affecting one of them or
the community as a whole.   In others certain decisions may
be made by the leader of the community, or by the staff
together, but in both situations the way decisions are
taken is visible to the whole community.   This contrasts
with the 'Kafkaesque' quality of many institutions where
decisions emanate from secret places and are then handed
down in such a manner that the recipient feels helpless to
do anything about it should he disagree: a situation

familiar both to staff and inmates of many traditional
institutions.

4 To provide a forum for personal 'feedback'; group meetings provide a situation where people can give and get personal reactions from one another, where participants can
learn how they are seen not just by one other person but by
many, and where as a result they can try to be less aggres-
sive/demanding/self-effacing, to listen more/take more
interest in others/or whatever change is suggested by the
others.

5 Allied to this, group meetings provide the vehicle for
community members to exert pressure on individuals whose
attitudes or behaviour are disturbing or upsetting to
others, or threaten his own well-being. This is going one
step further than simply giving feedback which the individual can choose to accept or ignore. In one community the
pressure might be in the form of an exortation, 'Why don't
you try asking more politely next time you want to watch
the other TV channel?' In another it might take the form
of being put on 'probation' in the community, or being
given a 'contract' to change a particular way of behaving.

Beyond these five common functions of group meetings, different types of therapeutic communities may employ other
methods of group therapy selected from the wide range of
techniques presently available including group analysis,
psychodrama, art therapy and family therapy.

The third element common to all therapeutic communities is
sharing the work of maintaining and running the community.
This may vary from, at one extreme, residents doing virtually
everything - cooking, cleaning, decorating, laundry, shopping,
administration - to the other where hospital patients may help
in serving meals and washing up but leave most of the chores
to paid staff. All therapeutic communities include some
degree of real work, that is, work which contributes to the
daily life of the community rather than work which is created
in order to occupy the patients. Such work is important for
several reasons.

1 Participating in the community's daily tasks helps members to feel part of the community, to feel it is their
community. By contributing to its upkeep they are recognised as valued members of the community.

2 People who have never learned to lead independent, res-

ponsible lives can begin to acquire the necessary skills
and confidence to use them.

3 Working with others in ordinary everyday tasks will
bring to light many interpersonal problems which might
remain dormant in group meetings.   Reluctance to share or
co-operate with someone else, fear of responsibility,
insistence on always doing things one's own way, lack of
persistence, may all emerge more clearly in a shared task
of work than in a group discussion.   Having emerged, these
difficulties can then be examined in group meetings.

4 In addition to its practical or therapeutic merits, participation in constructive work also has certain moral con-
notations.   One of the forerunners of therapeutic communities was 'moral treatment'.   This was created by social
reformers who saw regular productive work as one of the
main methods of treatment for the insane, helping to bring
them back to a normal life.   The inclusion of shared communal tasks in the daily programme of modern therapeutic
communities reflects not only their therapeutic value for
the individual, but also the moral values of social responsibility and good citizenship.

The fourth common feature is the recognition of patients or
residents as auxiliary therapists, commenting on and influencing each other's behaviour and attitudes.   Naturally this
goes on between the members of any community, even in the
wards of a general hospital, but often in an 'unofficial' way:
at mealtimes or during leisure activities.   In a therapeutic
community deliberate use is made of the effectiveness of this
informal source of influence.

Patients in a psychiatric therapeutic community are encouraged to take responsibility for thinking and deciding about
matters which affect not only themselves but their fellow
patients too.   New candidates for admission may be assessed
by a mixed group of staff and patients.   Once admitted,
patients assess their own and each others' progress.   Is Joan
ready to go and look for a job?   Should Roger visit his
parents this weekend?   Is Mary really depressed or is she
just trying to get all the attention?   When such questions
are discussed, for example in a community meeting, many processes are going on.   The person in focus is being confronted
with interpretations of his behaviour as it is seen by his own
peers, the other patients or residents.   Since some of them
may be in the same situation, they can understand the problems
and also see through excuses and false impressions.   Rapaport

called this the principle of Reality Confrontation. (5)   At
the same time the experience of taking a therapeutic role
towards others can help to develop self-confidence and self-
esteem which are often lacking in people with psychiatric or
emotional problems.   A further bonus is that patients may be
better at explaining things to fellow patients because they
use ordinary language rather than the jargon that professionals often use.

Linked to the role of auxiliary therapist is the more
general sharing of authority by staff and residents.   Residents are involved to a greater or lesser degree in the various decisions which have to be made in the running of the community.   These may include the planning of community activities such as cooking a meal, going on an outing, organising
sports and social events.   They may involve the relations
between the community and outsiders - how many visitors the
community can accommodate in one day, how to improve relationships with the neighbours.   They may concern matters of
income and expenditure - raising money for a new record
player, finding the cheapest place to buy food, deciding how
to spend a welcome donation.

Such decisions can be shared in different ways.   In communities which subscribe to an egalitarian form of power
sharing decisions may be made on the principle of one person-
one vote, regardless of status, or on the basis of a consensus
with attention being paid to the views of all.   In the latter
situation some members may be more influential than others,
but the principle is that everyone should have the opportunity
to take part in the decision-making process.   The other form
of sharing is a hierarchy in which certain decisions are dele-
gated downwards.   For instance, the director of a community
delegates responsibility for different tasks to junior staff,
who in turn delegate to residents the responsibility for such
activities as preparing meals or cleaning the house.   They in
turn may delegate particular jobs to others.   It is important
to recognise that although the first form may appear to be
more democratic, both represent ways of giving residents real
responsibility in relation to the day-to-day management of the
community.

So far the common attributes have been those concerned with
'practice' — with the daily events and routines of therapeutic
communities.   In addition to these there are certain 'values'
or beliefs which characterise such communities.   In saying
what these are I am aware that different types of therapeutic
communities may consider themselves to have different - even

opposing - values. We might find this, for example, if we
talked with members of 'democratic' and 'hierarchical' communities. Nevertheless it seems to me that it is possible to
identify some basic ideals or points of view that are shared
by all therapeutic communities.

First is the acceptance of some basic psychodynamic principles. One of these has been described as 'the belief inherent in most psychotherapy and psychological treatment that
an individual's difficulties are mostly in relation with other
people.' (6) The psychodynamic view of psychological symptoms such as anxiety or depression, or disorders of behaviour
such as delinquency and self-destructive acts, is that they
are the outward expression of emotional conflicts and tensions
in an individual's relations with others. This view, that
symptoms have meaning, that irrational behaviour can be
understood, stems from the work of Freud and psychoanalysis.
While many therapeutic communities do not follow psychoanalytic ideas as such, most would agree that one special advantage
of therapeutic communities is the opportunity they provide for
observing the connection between psychological disturbance in
an individual and changes in his relationships with others.

Another basic principle of psychodynamic therapies is that
therapy is essentially a learning process: both in the sense
of learning about oneself and others, and learning how to
relate to others, for example how to be more open or more
assertive. This view of therapy is fundamentally different
from the medical view in which the patient is a relatively
passive recipient of treatment, and 'cure' or 'failure' is
dependent upon the skill of the doctor and nurses. In a
therapeutic community, as in other forms of psychotherapy, the
process is more like that of education. The resident is in
the position of a learner, who benefits most when he is inter-
acting with the material to be learned. In this case the
material includes the other people in the community and the
individual's own thoughts and feelings.

Another shared value which characterises therapeutic communities is the recognition of the basic equality of all members, whether staff or residents, professionals or non-
professionals, therapists or patients. This equality has two
aspects, which may be called the human and the psychological.
By human equality I am referring to the belief that we should
treat others as we would like to be treated, that we should
not exploit others or unduly restrict their rights or freedom.
Where such freedoms are restricted - e.g. insistence on
attending group meetings, not allowing community members to

enter into a sexual relationship - this should be through the consensus of the community as being in the interests of the individuals affected or of the community as a whole.

The second equality is the recognition that all members, whatever their role, share many of the same psychological qualities. To put this in the context of a hospital, staff are not completely 'well' and patients are not completely 'sick'. Staff members can at times feel upset, anxious, or helpless; patients can at times be caring, creative, and competent. Neither side has a monopoly of strengths or weaknesses. This contrasts with the view found in more traditional hospitals, where staff and patients usually find it comfortable to adopt the complementary roles of helper and helpless, ignoring those parts of themselves that do not fit with these roles. This custom is so widespread in our society that it often occurs in therapeutic communities too, especially among new staff and patients.

This is not to suggest that in therapeutic communities there are no differences between the helpers and the helped, but rather that the other bits of oneself can also be shown. Staff members can admit to feelings which fall outside the conventional staff role - e.g. frustration or confusion - and patients can 'admit' to areas of skill and understanding that do not qualify as usual patient attributes.

The third common value is difficult to define and yet is important to appreciate if we are to understand what therapeutic communities are about. One thing of which newcomers are often aware is the sense of entering a 'closed order' to which they do not belong and where certain things are not open to question. For example, all the talk about openness and honesty may not seem to include permission to question the value of having a therapeutic community. Which is just what the newcomer often wants to do. While much of this feeling may be what a newcomer experiences in any situation, there is also a sense in which therapeutic communities do represent a moral value for those who work in them. By this I mean that the various principles and procedures described in this chapter have developed not only because they are considered to be therapeutically useful, but because they also express certain beliefs about relationships, about how people ought to treat each other, and in particular about how professional workers ought (and ought not) to treat their patients or clients.

Tom Main eloquently expressed such beliefs in the article which first introduced the term therapeutic community.

The anarchical rights of the doctor in the traditional
hospital society have to be exchanged for the more sincere
role of member in a real community, responsible not only to
himself and his superiors, but to the community as a whole,
privileged and restricted only insofar as the community
allows or demands. He no longer owns 'his' patients.
They are given up to the community which is to treat them,
and which owns them and him. Patients are no longer his
captive children, obedient in nursery-like activities, but
have sincere adult roles to play, and are free to reach for
responsibilities and opinions concerning the community of
which they are a part. (7)

Although most therapeutic communities are non-religious,
the existence of this moral component owes much to the strong
religious convictions of many therapeutic community pioneers.
In England Quakers have been responsible for many of the inno-
vations from which modern therapeutic communities derive,
while in America the origins of the concept-based communities
can be traced back to a radical Christian sect called the
Oxford Group.

The existence of a strong moral or ideological aspect to
therapeutic communities can be seen as both an asset and a
risk. It is an asset because it contributes to a high level
of enthusiasm and commitment among the staff and residents.
The instillation of hope and raising of morale are an important part of any therapeutic enterprise, and the moral value
which therapeutic community members attach to their approach
gives it a headstart in this respect. (8) The risk is that
moral valuing may slip over into idealisation of the community
and a refusal to listen to criticism or acknowledge limitations. There is a risk of therapeutic communities becoming
'Messianic', seeing themselves as guardians of the 'truth',
and the rest of the world as envious and malicious. Instan-
ces have arisen where communities have acquired these Messianic overtones, with destructive consequences for their members. (9) Learning to strike the right balance between moral
conviction and openness to self-appraisal is a difficult task
faced by all those who work in the helping professions. It
is a particularly difficult task in a therapeutic community,
where work and personal values are so closely bound up with
each other.

Chapter 2
The institutional therapeutic community

In countries as diverse as England, America, Israel and Cuba
there has emerged the concept of the therapeutic community
approach as an antidote to the effects of traditional institutional arrangements for the mentally ill. These arrangements
had become infamous for their regimentation and repression,
for the lack of initiative and individuality which they per-
mitted, for their purely custodial nature. In attempting to
change these institutions a handful of courageous hospital
superintendents envisioned a therapeutic community where
patients would take an active part in their own rehabilitation, relearning social and work skills long forgotten, and
where staff would facilitate, encourage and lead rather than
restrict, punish and prevent.

Such changes were not easily brought about, and the
efforts, even when successful, were not always lasting. A
therapeutic community is not a static piece of equipment but
a way of relating and communicating - never easy, never automatic, and always in danger of succumbing to administrative
convenience. Much has been written both about the traditional asylum-like institutions and about attempts to turn
them into therapeutic communities. In order to appreciate
the origins of the institutional therapeutic community, we
need to take a detour into the more distant history of psychiatry, for this is not the first time that its practitioners
have tried to overcome bad conditions and ineffective care.

MORAL TREATMENT

The background story to the idea of running an institution
for the mentally ill as a therapeutic community goes back to
the turn of the eighteenth and nineteenth centuries. It was

15

a time of widespread social upheaval: the American war of
Independence and the French Revolution were recent events,
and in England social reformers were active in championing the
rights of the underprivileged and oppressed.   In this context
there was a great interest in the welfare and treatment of the
'insane', who till that time had been lumped together with
other groups of social deviants unable to care for themselves
or regarded as a nuisance to society - vagrants, petty crimi-
nals, the physically handicapped and the destitute poor.
Such people were usually kept at home with their families, or
else in one of the custodial institutions of the time - the
poorhouse, the workhouse, the madhouse, the 'hospital' (a
medieval concept, ecclesiastical not medical) or the gaol.

Concern for the fate of mentally disturbed people, especially those confined to squalid madhouses where inmates were
sometimes kept chained to the wall, led to the development of
a new method of treatment known as moral treatment.   Despite
its rather - to modern ears - quaint name, moral treatment included many of the elements which today form part of the
essential basis of any therapeutic community - especially
those for the rehabilitation of long-term psychiatric
patients.

What is remarkable is that having made its appearance and
flourished for a few decades - until around the middle of the
nineteenth century - moral treatment then faded.   It disappeared into the brickwork, so to speak, of the very institutions which had been built largely in its name.   When therapeutic communities began making their appearance in large
mental hospitals in the years following the Second World War,
they were reviving a way of running those institutions that
had laid dormant for nearly a hundred years.   Three questions
are of interest to us here.   How did moral treatment come
about?   What was it?   Why did it disappear?

How did moral treatment come about?

When a Quaker patient died mysteriously in the York charity
asylum, the incident so disturbed the local Quaker community
that they decided to construct their own asylum for Friends
'deprived of the use of their reason'.   Founded and run by
William Tuke, a tea and coffee merchant, the York Retreat
opened in 1792.   It took about thirty patients.   Over the
next twenty years Tuke developed an approach that had a profound effect on the treatment of the insane as practised at
that time.   In place of physical restraints and enforced

idleness, common in eighteenth-century madhouses, he showed
how treating the insane as near as possible as normal people
and giving them useful occupations could produce unimagined
improvement in their mental state.   This approach came to be
known as moral treatment.   A term difficult to translate into
modern concepts, it implied the treatment of the character of
the individual, the whole person in his social environment.
Advocates of this new approach firmly believed that it was
best conducted away from the site of the original difficulties
- the insane person's home - in the calming sanctuary of a
well-run asylum.   The success of the Retreat was well publi-
cised and helped to set in motion intense debates about
existing institutions for the mentally ill.   Parliamentary
inquiries led to a series of laws which, by 1845, required
every county in England to provide for its 'pauper lunatics'
a purpose-built asylum.

Meanwhile visitors from other countries such as France and
America were so impressed by Tuke's work that they returned
home determined to publicise his ideas, and in 1817 a hospital
modelled on the York Retreat was founded in the United States
by the Pennsylvania Quakers.   But the situation in America
was very different from the one in England.   They did not
have the widespread tradition of private and charity institutions for social deviants that existed in England, the abuses
in which had led directly to the founding of the York Retreat.
The concerns of the new Americans, following the 1776 Declara-
tion of Independence, were to do with the creation of a new
type of society - the first democratic republic.   They wanted
to demonstrate to themselves and the rest of the world that
such social problems as crime and insanity could be overcome
in their new type of society.   Paradoxically, many Americans
believed that life in this new society of unlimited opportunities led to increased likelihood of mental breakdown.
Doctors warned that when people over-reached their capacities
the result was insanity.   For these doctors 'Moral Treatment'
meant placing the victim of these social pressures in an environment designed to restore his inner equilibrium.   In
their asylums they attempted to create a new, ideal mini-
society in which the virtues of order, calm and productive
work would replace the chaos and competitiveness of a burgeon-
ing new world. (1)

Thus for quite different reasons moral treatment caught on
in America and England in the early nineteenth century - in
England to counter the abuses of a long-established pattern of
containment in private madhouses and charity asylums, in
America to counter the distressing effects of contemporary

society on its more vulnerable members.   Although attempts to create Utopian communities were also taking place in England at this time, these had little to do with contemporary efforts to reform the treatment of the insane.   Indeed English reformers were themselves sceptical of the view that social conditions could cause insanity.   Yet despite their different beliefs about the causes of insanity, and despite their different motives for wanting to bring about a radical change in the treatment of the insane, the English and American reformers developed a remarkably similar approach.   In both countries the enthusiasm of the proponents of moral treatment led to an increasing number of asylums being built for the express purpose of conducting this form of treatment, and for a time it seemed as though the solution to insanity had been found.

What was moral treatment?

It can be described in three ways: as an ideology, as a practice, and as a set of principles about the treatment of mental illness.

Ideology

By ideology I mean the views about the way society ought to be organised, and about the consequences of organising it one way or another - in this case with particular reference to the treatment of insanity.   Two different ideologies supported the development of moral treatment, one in America and one in England.   American psychiatrists in the early nineteenth century believed that contemporary society was often psychologically harmful, and that the answer lay not in changing that society, but in creating asylums in which a new social order would 'rehabilitate the casualities of the system', by being designed 'in the reverse image of the world they had left'. Today the idea that a community created in the 'reverse image' of society at large can be therapeutic for the casualities of that society, is again a popular one, linking moral treatment with modern therapeutic communities.   In both, the logic is the same: if one kind of social environment produces mental distress, the opposite kind of social environment will heal it.   The difference is that whereas the creators of America's asylums ordered their communities in contrast to a chaotic society outside, many modern therapeutic communities are 'permissive' in contrast to a society that is felt to be too conforming and repressive.

A quite different ideology was espoused by Tuke.   Unlike
America, where moral treatment was pioneered by medical doctors, in England it developed as a challenge to the medical
profession, or at least to those doctors who profited by
claiming to be experts in the treatment of the insane.
Andrew Scull, in his book 'Museums of Madness' writes that,

Tuke had explicitly not sought to create or train a group
of experts in moral treatment.   He and his followers were
deeply suspicious of any plan to hand the treatment of
lunatics over to experts.   In the words of William Ellis
(the superintendent of one of the new moral treatment
asylums), 'Of the abuses that have existed, the cause of a
great proportion of them may be traced to the mystery with
which many of those who have had the management of the
insane have constantly endeavoured to envelope it.'   Those
who had developed moral treatment claimed that the new
approach was little more than an application of common
sense and humanity;   and these were scarcely qualities
monopolised by experts. (2)

In other words, the advocates of moral treatment in England
had an ideology which dispensed with 'expertise' on two
counts: it had been used to conceal harmful practices, and it
was unnecessary because what the insane needed could be given
by anyone with the right attitude and personal qualities.

The emergence of the therapeutic community movement was
accompanied by very similar arguments.   Tom Main, in the
first published account of a therapeutic community in 1946,
wrote that the doctor had to give up his 'anarchical rights'
in exchange for 'the more sincere role of member in a real
community'.   The recent popularity of the writings of Ronald
Laing and Ivan Illich indicate that such ideological questions
as 'what kind of society is best for the emotional health of
its members?' and 'how much should we let experts take over
our problems?' are once more of concern to many people. (3)

Practice

The basic nature of moral treatment sounds simple enough to
our ears: engage the patients in a regular routine of useful,
varied work, and do this within an intimate, family-like
atmosphere in an attractive setting and location.   Yet this
at the time was revolutionary.   Prior to moral treatment the
institutions for the insane had been noted for the enforced
idleness of inmates who were often chained or manacled, and

lived in filthy overcrowded cells, where the smell could make
a visitor vomit.   The pioneers of moral treatment in England
intended to show that physical restraint was rarely needed
and that insanity was curable not by any of the then current
medical treatments such as bleeding or purging, but by ordinary employment in everyday tasks, which restored order and
tranquillity to men's minds.   These included farming, gardening, household tasks and simple workshop tasks.   The particular task mattered less than the way it was carried out.   A
precise and regular routine would bring order to disordered
lives.   Regular employment would encourage patients in self-
restraint, take their minds off their problems, and encourage
the regular work habits which would turn them into productive
members of society.

Equally important was the atmosphere in which these activities were carried out.   Patients were treated as normal,
rational beings.   Staff tolerated disturbed behaviour as
much as possible, and used solitude or physical restraint
only as a last resort.   The overall atmosphere was meant to
resemble an extended family, with the asylum superintendent
as its head.   The role of the superintendent was of central
importance.

By paying minute attention to all aspects of the day-to-
day conduct of the institution, by always setting through
his example a high standard for subordinates to emulate in
their dealing with the inmates, he could foster the kind
of intimate and benevolent familiar environment in which
acts of violence would naturally become rare. (4)

Principles

The curability of insanity.   Prior to the era of moral
treatment it was generally assumed that madness was incurable.
Beliefs about its cause varied: the will of God, possession
by evil spirits, a hereditary disease passed on through the
blood.   The attitude to treatment was in all cases the same.
Once struck, the unfortunate victim could only be cared for
or, if dangerous, sent away or locked up.   Occasional physical remedies were applied by doctors, of the kind applied to
patients with fever, but the results were not encouraging.
The single greatest change brought about by moral treatment
was the new belief, and the demonstration, that insanity was
curable, and that its cure lay not in the erudite realm of
medicine but in the everyday realm of the patient's daily
routine and social environment.   The achievement was not so

much in finding a cure, as in changing the task of the asylum from custody to rehabilitation.   It was a change which would have to be repeated in later years.

Reward rather than punish.   The moral treatment pioneers acted on the assumption that patients were amenable to social inducements to behave acceptably, to the praise, encouragement and the esteem of others.   Severe discipline and harsh restraints were not only inhumane, they were unnecessary. Patients would respond according to the staff's expectations: treat them as uncontrollable madmen and that is how they will behave, treat them as rational, responsible beings and they will act accordingly.   One measure of this change of approach was the amazement of visitors to the new asylums on seeing patients allowed to handle knives and sharp farm implements. The success of moral treatment as a new and better way of treating the mentally ill - not only more humane but more effective - was repeatedly emphasised by its advocates. Recent critics of moral treatment, like Scull, have also pointed out that it was a method of moulding patients into the kind of citizens that suited society.   He wrote:

> The insane were to be restored to reason by a system of rewards and punishment not essentially different from those used to teach a young child to obey the dictates of 'civilised' morality ... the lunatics were to be made over in the image of bourgeois rationality: defective human mechanisms were to be repaired so that they could once more compete in the marketplace. (4)

Today the same criticisms can be and are made of therapeutic communities - and of other forms of psychiatric treatment too - that they bring about social conformity.   What such critics neglect to add is that it is very difficult for an individual to live in society without conforming to its basic norms and values.

The importance of size and setting.   In order to create an intimate family-like atmosphere the number of inmates and staff in an asylum had to be kept small.   The ideal was considered to be a total of between 100 and 120 - at most 200 - divided into units of about ten people.   This would correspond to a large extended family, small enough for patients to have all the individual care they required, and all be personally known to the superintendent.   Moral treatment could not be carried out, its advocates argued, when the numbers in an asylum grew too large for an intimate, family atmosphere to exist.   These warnings were not heeded, as we shall see.

The reformers in England and America also believed that the physical construction and setting of the asylum was crucial to the success of treatment.   So much so, in fact, that many medical superintendents became obsessed with the details of building and design.   They required the asylum to be located far away from the disturbing influence of city life, in a soothing rustic setting with pleasant views and walks.   Since they believed that the patient's social environment - usually a town or city - had contributed to his breakdown, it was logical to them that recovery required as big a separation from this environment as possible.   For the same reason visits from friends and relatives were generally discouraged. It is interesting to realise that these are the reasons why nineteenth-century mental hospitals were located away from centres of population, since today we often assume that this was solely in order to rid city dwellers of having the insane in their midst.

The personal attributes of the staff.   Moral treatment lay great emphasis on having enough staff to give individual care to patients.   In the better establishments they numbered as many as one for every four or five patients.   It was recognised that the attendant was the person who had the most extensive and intimate contact with the patient.   His personal qualities were therefore of great importance, and the new superintendent paid a lot of attention to selecting the right kind of staff.   They had to be kind, intelligent, of upright character and with an unusual degree of forbearance.   There was apparently no shortage of suitable applicants.   Young men and women of respectable families, adequate education and 'refined moral feelings' were often prepared to devote a few years to asylum employment.   Today it is again true that young, well-educated people are often attracted to work in therapeutic communities, as assistants or social therapists. Compared with the years before, and immediately following moral treatment, it was an era of remarkable social responsiveness to the needs of the mentally ill.

Why did moral treatment disappear?

Many reasons have been put forward to explain why this humane and apparently successful approach should have all but vanished by the time the last county asylums were being built in the 1890s.   No one explanation alone will do, and it would be hard to say which, if any, was the decisive one.   In one sense, it was killed by its own success as a reform movement. Social reformers, pointing to the success of the early

attempts at moral treatment, persuaded the English Parliament
and the American States to provide similar institutions on an
increasingly large scale.   But in doing so they ignored the
vital matter of the size of the asylum.   In order to cater
for all the insane - not only those in madhouses but those
presently looked after by their families - an upper limit of
200 was stretched to 300, then to 500, then 1,000 and finally
vast mental hospitals containing 2-3,000 patients were constructed.   With such numbers the aim of establishing a family
atmosphere was left far behind.

The type of patient began to change too.   In the middle
decades of the nineteenth century both America and its asylums
were flooded with poor immigrants who were arriving from
Europe.   The goal of creating a stable, well-ordered society
became increasingly remote, both within and outside the
asylum.   In England a law passed in 1890 required that only
the most incurable should be admitted to hospital.   Such
changes tended to push asylums towards a more custodial role
on both sides of the Atlantic.

One aspect of moral treatment which survived only too well
in the new asylums was the emphasis on supervision and inspection.   Originally this had been introduced to ensure that
the abuses of the madhouse were not repeated and that atten-
dants were treating patients with proper tolerance and encouragement.   But supervision in a personal, family-like
setting is very different from supervision in a large institution.   Shorn from its original role as one part of moral
treatment, inspection grew to be an all-pervading obsession
in many large asylums.

Another reason has been suggested by Scull to account for
the decline of moral treatment, especially as practised by
non-medically qualified people.   The reluctance of Tuke and
his followers to establish a new profession of 'experts' in
moral treatment meant that there was no coherent body to challenge the claim of the medical profession to responsibility
for the mentally ill.   As the original pioneers retired,
died or became disillusioned, their efforts died with them.
Disillusion must have been produced not only by the increasing
size of the institutions but also by the discovery in the
latter half of the nineteenth century that many of the earlier
claims to success had been exaggerated.   This had the effect
of discrediting what success had been achieved.   Meanwhile
different views of the nature of mental illness were beginning
to prevail.   Interest was shifting to a search for organic
causes, and although this search was relatively unsuccessful,

it left moral treatment with its emphasis on social factors as an outmoded and apparently discredited approach.

THE EMERGENCE OF THE INSTITUTIONAL THERAPEUTIC COMMUNITY

By the end of the nineteenth century all that was left of the era of moral treatment was a collection of asylums whose size alone condemned them to a life of routine and regimentation. With the passing of moral treatment so too passed the belief in the treatability of mental illness. The country air and the views, once thought beneficial for the mentally disturbed town dweller, now ensured that his plight was forgotten by all except those who had direct contact with the institution. The world of the asylum changed little in the first half of the twentieth century. Attempts were made in the 1930s by some Dutch and English psychiatrists to introduce work pro- grammes to counteract the effects of institutional boredom and lethargy. But in 1956 a Boston psychiatrist named J.S. Bockoven described a ward in an American mental hospital as follows:

> It is not until one enters the wards where the patients live that one feels the impact of what it means to be a patient in a typical mental hospital. Contrary to one's expectations, ward after ward may be passed through without witnessing the violent, the grotesque, or the ridiculous. Instead, one absorbs the heavy atmosphere of hundreds of people doing nothing and showing interest in nothing. Endless lines of people sit on benches along the walls. Some have their eyes closed; others gaze fixedly at the floor or the opposite wall. Occasionally a head is turned to look out of a window or to watch someone coming back from the toilet to take his place on a bench. All in all, it is an innocuous scene characterised by inertness, list- lessness, docility, and utter hopelessness.

The attitude of the staff reveals a faint and distorted echo from the days of moral treatment:

> The visitor learns that the attendant is proud of the ward because it is quiet and no mishaps have occurred while he was on duty; because the floor is clean; because the patients are prompt and orderly in going to and from meals. The visitor finds that the scene which appalls him with the emptiness and pointlessness of human life is regarded by the attendant as good behaviour on the part of the patients.

In other countries the situation was worse than this. An
account of the main mental hospital in Havana before the Cuban
Revolution in 1959 describes the patients as 'herded up naked
and hungry, lacking hygiene and the necessary food'. (5)
Patients and convicts were mixed in together, a situation
still to be found in countries which do not distinguish
between different types of social deviance. The film 'Mid-
night Express' portrays such conditions - similar to those
which existed in Britain and America before moral treatment -
still existing in at least one European country in recent
years.

The attempt to apply therapeutic community principles in
large mental hospitals was the result of a number of forces
which converged together in Britain in the 1950s. To begin
with there were a handful of hospital superintendents who had
tried to overcome their hospitals' custodial role although
falling short of a complete reorganisation of the institution.
At Dingleton hospital the doors to the wards were unlocked;
at Mapperly the nurses began to work with patients outside the
hospital; at Warlingham Park a superintendent knowledgeable
of the history of moral treatment, T.P. Rees, encouraged
junior psychiatrists to conduct group meetings on the wards.
Two of them, Bertram Mandelbrote and Denis Martin, went on to
play leading roles in the application of therapeutic community
principles in large institutions. (6)

The institutional therapeutic community was more than a
simple re-emergence of moral treatment. Four other factors
played an important part. One was the example provided by
the new, small, specialised therapeutic communities which had
developed during and since the Second World War and which are
discussed later. The leaders of these small units, which
selected their patients carefully, did not always think that
their methods were applicable to the chronic psychotic
patients in large mental hospitals. Nevertheless, hospital
superintendents like Mandelbrote, Martin and Clark probably
felt they had little to lose and much to gain by trying out
these methods in the large, traditional institutions of which
they had assumed leadership.

A second influence was the emergence of a trend related to
therapeutic communities - group therapy. Two psychoanalysts
who had become interested in leading groups in the course of
the wartime therapeutic community experiments (described in
the next chapter) continued to exert a significant influence
on mental health workers in the post-war years. W.R. Bion
led study groups at the Tavistock Clinic and S.H. Foulkes was

appointed psychotherapist at the Maudsley Hospital, London's
leading psychiatric teaching hospital. Psychiatrists training there had the opportunity to gain first-hand group experience which they were later able to use in getting patients and
staff to meet and discuss their mutual concerns.

A third important force in this period of rethinking about
asylums was the sociological research in American psychiatric
hospitals by Stanton and Schwartz, Caudill, and Goffman.
They studied the social behaviour of inmates in mental hospitals. They observed how an unexpressed conflict between members of staff on a ward could lead to disturbed behaviour
amongst the patients, how failure to deal openly with a source
of collective tension may result in mutual withdrawal of
patients and staff and then an outbreak of collective disturbance, how the relationships among patients and between staff
and patients may be understood in terms of the social effects
of living in what Goffman called a 'total institution' - where
every aspect of life takes place within the asylum.

Not only were these studies fascinating, they also provided
a rationale for trying to change the way the institutions were
run.   Above all they showed the importance of open communica-
tions in order to avoid the build-up of tension around hidden
issues of conflict.   They also indicated that behaviour could
be explained in terms of how patients and staff adjusted to
the social 'system' of the hospital, not just in terms of
individual illness or personality.   To change people, then,
it might be necessary to understand and change the social
organisation of the ward or hospital.

Such ideas gave impetus to the therapeutic community
approach.   In England impetus also came from the creation in
1948 of the National Health Service.   There was a challenge
to do something about the seemingly untreatable chronic
schizophrenics who filled the mental hospitals in their thou-
sands, and there were the resources and enthusiasm to make
things work.   It may not be a coincidence that the therapeutic community approach to asylum populations has often been
tried in the wake of wider social changes.   Moral treatment
itself arose in the wake of the American and French revolu-
tions.   Cuba and Israel provide two recent examples of new
societies with new approaches to traditional problems.   The
creation of a national health service falls short of total
revolution, but perhaps provides an essential ingredient - the
belief that a new approach can overcome problems that the old
'regime' had found insoluble.

THE INSTITUTIONAL THERAPEUTIC COMMUNITY IN PRACTICE

Today many large psychiatric hospitals have introduced methods
which blend together the old principles of moral treatment and
recent therapeutic community ideas. Group meetings, patient
responsibility, a belief in the goals of rehabilitation, these
are some of the common features of such hospitals. Yet
unlike the small specialised therapeutic communities, these
hospitals contain mostly chronic psychiatric patients who have
either been in hospital for many years or can only live outside with continuing support and occasional readmission.
Some patients may act or think in bizarre ways, others may be
peaceable but apathetic and withdrawn. The goal for such
patients is often to help them lead a daily pattern of living
which corresponds to a conventional idea of normality - getting up, going to work or some other regular activity, eating
meals which they may have helped to prepare, getting on with
the people they live with, and so on.

One of the hallmarks of a therapeutic community is a breaking down of the distinction between staff and patient roles
which exist in traditional treatment settings, where staff
decide and patients abide. In therapeutic communities for
the chronic mentally ill the staff still do decide many
things. The delegation to patients of responsibilities for
making decisions, organising activities, helping in each
others' treatment, is real but limited. The goals described
above are still determined in a largely conventional manner
by the doctor or staff team. If the goals were determined
democratically many patients would probably vote to retain the
institutional pattern of living to which they had become
accustomed. Limitations also arise because some patients
lack the necessary skills and capacities for active participation in running a community, and because staff who have been
accustomed to a traditional helping role may still prefer to
do things for patients. For all these reasons institutional
therapeutic communities are likely to differ from those which
originally gave rise to the term, in which patients (or residents) are able to take responsibilities on a par with those
of the staff.

It is important to recognise its limitations if we are to
avoid having too high expectations of the aims of the institutional therapeutic community. Yet within these limitations
patients can and do take on roles which are quite beyond those
found in traditional mental hospitals, and staff involvement
and morale may take on a new, fresher complexion.

A major innovation when changing an institution towards a
therapeutic community way of working is the creation of small
living and working groups of ten or so patients. In contrast
to the trivial, repetitive tasks that are frequently used to
occupy patients' time in traditional psychiatric hospitals,
the work has some real and apparent values. It may include
the chores of domestic living, or outside work of a practical
nature such as gardening, farmwork, building, carpentry, etc.
Patients who are capable of it are encouraged to take responsibility for the way the work is organised and may assume the
roles of foreman or instructor.

Group meetings form an important part of these communities
- although not as frequent as in other types of therapeutic
communities. Community meetings of the whole ward or unit,
staff and patients, will probably take place once or twice a
week, focusing on issues arising in the day-to-day life of
the ward. These may include problems at work, incidents on
the ward, grievances felt by a patient towards another patient
or member of staff, patients' queries about their medication,
and so on. An additional purpose from the staff's point of
view is that these meetings can enable patients to learn to
talk about their feelings rather than act on them impulsively,
and may encourage patients to take upon themselves some of the
tasks of leadership in the meeting and in the ward as a whole.
Smaller group meetings also take place, usually linked to
particular tasks or activities. Patients are often encouraged to assess each other's work and discuss their feelings
about working together.

An arrangement which has special value in this kind of
therapeutic community is bringing together staff and patients
with people from the outside community, in particular
patients' relatives and prospective employers. For example,
these 'outsiders' may be invited to attend community meetings
or come for special meetings. The goals are two-fold: to
ease the anxieties that the 'outsiders' may have about the
way patients behave by letting them see for themselves; and
to help patients feel less isolated from the outside world by
gradually bringing them into contact with parts of it. This
process is often extended by the use of 'in between' living
situations so that the move from hospital to independent
living is not accomplished in a single, sudden change.
Patients may go to work from the hospital, or move out of
hospital to a supervised hostel and then to a group home where
four or five ex-patients live together with minimal supervision.

Last and in some ways most important are the meetings for
staff members. They are particularly important because the
staff may not all have chosen to work in this way. This
situation occurs, for example, when a new doctor introduces a
therapeutic community approach into a traditional ward or
hospital. It can also arise when part of an institution
operates as a therapeutic community but the institution as a
whole is run on more traditional lines, staff in the various
disciplines being allocated to wards in ways which take little
account of the orientation of particular units or individuals.* In either situation staff members can find themselves suddenly expected to work in a way that they have no
experience of and to which they may even be opposed. They
may be used to working in a clear-cut professional hierarchy
with little opportunity for free discussion between people at
the top and bottom of the hierarchy. Even less will they
expect patients to take an active part in organising their
own rehabilitation. An important part of the work in this
type of therapeutic community therefore lies in persuadingg
all the staff to accept and use the approach.

Only if the staff team as a whole believes that patients
are capable of independent, responsible behaviour, and that
regular meetings with open discussion of ward issues are
useful, will the therapeutic community flourish.

A doctor in Israel found that in establishing a therapeutic community for chronic psychiatric patients he needed
to persuade the staff to accept a number of new attitudes
towards the patients: that they could live in an open
institution, that they could have a favourable prognosis,
that drug therapy was only one part of treatment, and that
the mentally ill had a right to understanding and respect
as well as compassion. (7)

The staff meeting is vital for influencing staff attitudes,
for discussion of the problems and anxieties that arise from
day to day, and as an actual demonstration that open discussion of different viewpoints is both possible and helpful.

* One of the issues to be confronted in starting a therapeutic community in a ward in a large hospital is often the practice of moving nurses from ward to ward to meet requirements
for nursing cover. Nurse managers may be reluctant to give
priority to the need for staff continuity unless they understand and support the new approach.

In addition to their programme of work and group activities, most institutional therapeutic communities use the major tranquillising drugs to control the psychotic elements in patients' thinking, such as delusions, thought disorder, and extremes of mood.   Medication is regarded as the indispensable background which enables such patients to participate in the social activities of a therapeutic community.   This emphasises that therapeutic communities for the chronic mentally ill are not seen as a complete alternative to conventional treatment but as a way of organising a ward or hospital so as to maximise the possibilities for rehabilitation.

A distinctive feature of this type of therapeutic community is that the benefit is often not just to the patients but the whole institution.   The change from a custodial regime to one that aims to rehabilitate patients can bring with it a change from a dreary, monotonous atmosphere to one that is lively and enthusiastic, where staff are interested and involved.   It is this change in the atmosphere of the ward or hospital that some consider to be the most important change, bringing with it new goals and expectations of what can be achieved, greater compassion and tolerance in staff attitudes towards patients, and greater respect for patients' individuality. (8)

Looked at from this point of view a variety of different specific techniques may produce similar changes.   In the past fifteen years another approach has become widely used in the rehabilitation of chronic psychiatric patients;   the token economy, or behaviour modification programme.   This approach differs from the therapeutic community in that patients' behaviour is seen in terms of separate items which the staff monitor and influence through the use of rewards. These may be tokens which can be exchanged for goods at the hospital shop, or more personal rewards such as praise and encouragement.   Although it can be applied to numbers of patients the method is essentially individual.   Yet in some important respects it resembles the process in a therapeutic community.   Both approaches reflect a belief in the possibility of change in the chronic psychiatric patient, both approaches stimulate a high level of staff interest and involvement, and both increase the amount of interaction between staff and patients.

Instead of being seen as alternative approaches, it is possible that in working with chronic psychiatric patients the therapeutic community and the behaviour modification programme may come to be seen as complementary.   Behavioural approaches emphasise the precise details of individual behaviour which

sometimes get overlooked in a therapeutic community. The
therapeutic community approach emphasises social interaction
and the mutual support which patients can give to one another.
A combination of these two approaches offers interesting possibilities.

Chapter 3
Democracy and psychoanalysis

Moral treatment got as far as providing a humane, caring,
intimate environment in which disturbed or troublesome individuals were treated with normal dignity and encouraged to
lead orderly, productive lives. As we have seen, these
gains were lost in psychiatry and had to be regained. But
beyond this humane paternalism two ideas have gripped the
imagination of many twentieth-century pioneers working with
the disturbed, the difficult and the deviant: participative
democracy and psychoanalysis. In the quite different settings of schools for maladjusted children, psychiatric hospitals for adults who are emotionally disabled, and prisons for
youthful, aggressive offenders, these pioneers have created
regimes which bear a striking resemblance to one another.

Most widely shared has been the idea of giving the residents or inmates responsibility for deciding how they want
the establishment to be run and then working out with them
how this is to be done. This sharing of responsibility can
achieve several goals. It undermines the expectation of
being told what to do. Such an expectation tends to lead
either to compliance or to rebellion, neither of which is
helpful when the aim is for people to become more mature,
responsible individuals. It also allows people to learn in
a practical way the consequences of their decisions; and it
brings them into a situation where in order to get things
done they have to begin to co-operate with others, to see
other people's points of view and to know how to put their
own across in a reasonable way.

Such an approach provides enormous opportunities for increasing self-awareness and social maturity, yet it probably
could not have come about before nineteenth-century morality
had begun to yield to more liberal ideas. Four factors were

important in counteracting the repressive Victorian response
to social maladjustment and deviance. Two were not new: the
Christian ideal of love of the person, no matter how bad the
deed; and the democratic ideal of a republic in which all men
are equal. These two ideals were provided with an invaluable
ally in psychoanalysis, which emerged around the turn of the
twentieth century and showed how irrational behaviour could
be understood and, through understanding, changed. A fourth
factor was the impetus which the Second World War gave to in-
novations in psychiatry that might not have arisen in less
urgent times.

The term 'therapeutic community' was first used to describe
experiments which took place at a military psychiatric hospital during the early 1940s. However, many of the ingredients
of these experiments had already been tried out with maladjusted children under the heading of 'planned environment
therapy'. Although not identical there are sufficient similarities between planned environment therapy and therapeutic
communities to warrant our devoting some attention to the
former. Since both have been influenced by psychoanalysis,
it may be helpful to spend a page or two getting acquainted
with this subject.

THE CONTRIBUTION OF PSYCHOANALYSIS

Psychoanalysis was created by Freud in the last decade of the
nineteenth century both as a method for treating neuroses and
as a way of investigating unconscious thoughts, feelings and
experience. Both involved the method of free-association,
in which the patient was encouraged to say whatever came into
his mind. In therapeutic communities this has its equivalent
in the principle of permissiveness - allowing patients a wide
range of freedom in their actions. Psychoanalysis also produced, and continues to elaborate in its various 'schools', a
number of theories about the way personality develops. Im-
portantly from our point of view this brought a change in
attitudes towards social deviance and maladjustment, replac-
ing authoritarian and punitive attitudes with ones which
stressed empathy and understanding. Others too had stressed
the need for love and understanding, but psychoanalysis provided a more complete theory about what it was that needed
understanding. Those therapeutic community pioneers who in-
tuitively leant towards an equal sharing of roles and the
mutual discussion of problems in living, found in theories of
Freud and his contemporaries a powerful rationale to support
and guide their efforts. They also found a number of speci-

fic ideas which could either be applied 'straight' or adapted
to the particular needs of a therapeutic community.

   Broadly, psychoanalytic ideas have been made use of in
three ways.   The simplest application has been the practice
of individual psychotherapy within a therapeutic community.
The second has been the use of psychoanalytic concepts as a
way of understanding and using individual relationships
throughout the community.   The third has been a psychoanalytic approach to processes affecting the community as a whole,
for example, relationships between different sections of the
community or between the community and the world outside it.
Let us briefly consider each of these applications, and some
of the concepts involved.

   1 Psychoanalysis as a therapeutic method refers to a well-
   defined arrangement in which the psychoanalyst and patient
   meet together at a regular time three, four or five times
   a week, usually over a period of some years.   The psychoanalyst participates in a relationship with the patient in
   which the patient is encouraged to say (or, if a child, to
   do) whatever comes into his mind.   The application of this
   method has been used in a small number of therapeutic communities for maladjusted children for whom a close relationship with an adult is needed before they can begin to
   relate to other children.   It is only rarely applied in
   adult therapeutic communities, where it is the community
   with all its potential relationships which provides the
   therapy.

   2 Relationships between the members of a therapeutic community are subject to a number of distorting influences
   which interfere with members' capacity to work together
   and enjoy one another's company.   Many of these distor-
   tions can be attributed to involuntary psychological habits
   of thinking and feeling which members carry around with
   them, causing them to react inappropriately to people they
   meet.   When these habits emerge in relationships in the
   community there is an opportunity to examine, understand,
   and change them.   Several psychoanalytic concepts are used
   in this process of understanding.   'Transference' refers
   to a relationship in which one person attributes to
   another qualities which belong in the person's relationships with important others, usually family members.
   'Countertransference' refers to the emotions experienced
   towards that person by those to whom the transference is
   directed. (1)   For example, someone who often felt dis-
   approved of as a child may react to a new acquaintance -

in this case another member of the community - as though
they too were disapproving. His resulting behaviour might
be to try to win approval, which in turn will provoke a reaction, say of irritation in the new acquaintance. Such a
'countertransference' may confirm the original transference, setting up a chain or spiral of reactions. The concepts of transference and countertransference are valuable
aids in understanding what otherwise might appear only as a
difficult and inescapable 'vicious circle' between two or
more people.

A widow in her late fifties was admitted to hospital in
a depressed, withdrawn state. There had been difficulties between her and her son and two daughters, and they
did not come to visit her in hospital. She started to
complain that the staff were treating her badly. She
refused to attend community meetings and on several
occasions left the unit with the intention of walking
home, a journey of several miles, in bad weather.
Those staff who were most involved in containing her
began to feel increasingly frustrated and exasperated,
and found themselves becoming angry and unsympathetic
towards her. This reaction confirmed her belief that
she was being treated badly by the staff. When her
children were persuaded to start visiting her she
became much brighter and co-operative, and the staff
felt relieved and warmer towards her.

Another source of interference in personal relationships
occurs when one person attributes to another his own feelings or attitudes. This is called 'projection'. This
usually occurs when a person has a feeling which, in his
own eyes at least, is unacceptable. For example, if someone feels annoyed with you, instead of recognising this he
may instead perceive you as being annoyed with him.

Sometimes it happens that several people in a group or
community project some unacceptable quality into one individual who is then attacked and driven out. This is known
as 'scapegoating'. Often the individual concerned does
possess the unacceptable quality to some degree, which on
the surface can make the scapegoating seem reasonable.
For example, an individual with a propensity for violent
outbursts may be treated by everyone else as if he were the
only person with a problem in controlling his anger, enab-
ling others to ignore their own violent impulses. At
times such occurrences may have their constructive side, as
when a member of the community is confronted by the others

over his antisocial behaviour.   Being alert to the possibility of projection and scapegoating can help to reduce
their harmful effects, and may enable people to become more
aware of their own feelings.

The staff team of a therapeutic community was character-
ised by a casual, almost cavalier attitude towards
administrative forms and recordkeeping.   A new staff
member, more meticulous by nature, complained about the
lack of support she got in trying to organise things in
a more orderly way.   The staff responded by confronting
the new member about being over-conscientious and authoritarian.   In a staff meeting it was pointed out that,
while this had some truth, the other staff members had
anxieties about their own administrative roles which
were not being discussed.

3 We have now touched on the third use of psychoanalytic
concepts, when they are applied to the community as a
whole.   Psychological interactions may occur between one
section of the community and another, or between the community and outsiders.   An example of this is the use of
stereotypes: 'the staff don't care', 'the patients avoid
taking responsibility', 'the women object to swearing',
and so on.   Such stereotypes are often associated with
'splitting'.   This concept refers to what happens when one
group of people (usually called 'we' - e.g. 'we patients',
'we the senior staff') is seen as representing good qualities, such as sensitivity and understanding, while the
other group ('them') is seen as representing the opposite,
lack of understanding, high-handedness, etc.   This may
also arise between the 'we' of the community and the 'them'
of people outside, especially people with some influence
over the community.   Such splits can have a marked effect
on personal relationships, since they hinder the apprecia-
tion of other people's points of view as individuals.
The attempt to understand and examine such collective processes has probably been the most distinctive and original
application of psychoanalysis to therapeutic communities. (2)

PLANNED ENVIRONMENT THERAPY FOR CHILDREN AND ADOLESCENTS

The first attempt to combine psychoanalytic ideas with participative democracy took place in the field of therapeutic
education. (3)   At the turn of the twentieth century
there were in America a number of communities for disturbed

youngsters known as Junior Republics. These were modelled
on the United States constitution, with a president, legisla-
tive assembly, and so on, all posts being occupied by the
young inmates. The rationale was that since the United
States was a great nation, the treatment of delinquents in
self-governing institutions based on its constitution could
not help but succeed. One such 'republic' had been run by a
man called Homer Lane, and in 1913 he was invited to England
to advise on the setting up of a home for post-schoolage
delinquent adolescents.

Although Lane had run a Junior Republic he was rather more
psychologically sophisticated in his view of delinquency,
seeing it as a product of emotional deprivation. His fundamental belief was in the Christian ideal of love, believing
in the innate and spontaneous goodness of the child no matter
how bad the behaviour. He also possessed considerable
charisma and is widely regarded as the most influential
pioneer of the principle of self-government for treating disturbed adolescents. Although he was not the first to introduce it he was the first to apply it so completely and so
genuinely.

The community he ran was called the Little Commonwealth,
and the forty or so adolescent boys and girls and small team
of staff were its 'citizens'. Lane wrote:

The chief point of difference between the Commonwealth and
other reformatories is that in the Commonwealth there are
no rules and regulations except those made by the boys and
girls themselves ... the adult element studiously avoid
any assumption of authority in the community except in
connection with their duties as teachers or supervisors of
labour. [The individual and whole community were free]
to make mistakes, to test for themselves the value of
every law and the necessity for every restraint imposed
upon them.

Today we might describe this as a permissive atmosphere.

An interesting feature of the Little Commonwealth was
Lane's 'economic scheme'. The citizens were paid for doing
domestic and farm work in the community and were then charged
for their lodging, food, clothes, etc. If someone had not
earned enough to pay for his needs, the other citizens were
charged for him. This led to considerable pressure on individuals to behave responsibly towards the community. There
was also a Citizens' Court, in which all the members met

together to hear complaints about work or conduct and to award punishments. Lane considered that the confrontation of individuals by the group was one of the main forms of therapy in the community.

Psychoanalysis entered into the Little Commonwealth in a rather unfortunate way. While working in England, Lane became enthusiastic about the work of Freud and decided to apply it as a therapeutic technique with some of the girls in his care. By all accounts they enjoyed it, but allegations of sexual impropriety were made which led to the withdrawal of government support for the school. In 1918 the Little Commonwealth closed. The lesson was learnt by his successors, who with few exceptions did not venture to combine the roles of school head and psychotherapist.

In the 1920s and 1930s a number of pioneer educationalists, some inspired by their contact with Homer Lane, took up the cause of creating liberal therapeutic regimes for delinquent or difficult children. Although they differed in their personal styles, they were all trying to get away from the authoritarian, punitive attitudes of conventional reformatories, and from conventional notions about child-adult relationships in schools generally. One of these pioneers, A.S. Neill, went on to become famous for his many books on liberal education, and for his school, Summerhill, founded in 1924, which still survives, now run by his widow. Others created schools in the 1930s which have become legendary in the history of therapeutic work with maladjusted children, among them George Lyward at Finchden Manor, Otto Shaw at Red Hill School, and David Wills at the Hawkspur Camp.

Today these ventures, and many of their successors, are described under the broad heading of planned environment therapy. Despite this different name they have much in common with therapeutic communities. Indeed in many respects planned environment therapy is to maladjusted children what therapeutic communities are to psychiatrically disturbed adults. Both stem from a belief in the therapeutic benefits of delegating to the patient or pupil many of the responsibilities normally taken by staff, in an atmosphere which encourages open expression of feelings and exploration of relationships. Rules and punishments imposed by the staff are rejected in favour of discipline which emerges from the community as a whole, or from the spontaneous relationships between its members.

The man whose work originally gave body to the term

planned environment therapy was David Wills, whose ideas were
also probably closest to those of the therapeutic community.
More than other pioneers in this field, his work was of a co-
operative nature.   His chief collaborator was a doctor,
Marjorie Franklin, who through her work in mental hospitals
in the 1920s had become interested in the relationship between
mental illness and the patients' environment.   She wanted to
set up special camps for delinquent youths which could demonstrate the benefits of self-government as an educational or
therapeutic experience.   In 1934 she created a committee of
experts to set up and support such 'Q' camps (Q for quest or
query), and in David Wills she found the ideal leader for
these camps.

Wills, like Tuke, a Quaker, had been inspired by Homer
Lane, sharing his belief in the therapeutic value of love and
shared responsibility, but not his interest in practising
psychoanalytic therapy.   The first Q camp was established at
Hawkspur Green in 1936, for delinquent boys aged 16-19.   In
addition to Wills leading the camp there was a Selection and
Treatment Committee, and the use of outside treatment
experts.   This ensured that the style and success of the Q
camps were not solely dependent on the work of one person, a
weakness of many pioneer schools which closed or changed
following the leaders' death or departure.

Wills's concept of love embraces a number of beliefs: no
matter how obnoxious a child's appearance, habits or disposi-
tion, he or she is basically good and worthy of love and
affection;   punishment should never be used to correct or
influence a child's behaviour;   the domination of one person
or group by another is abhorrent - relationships should be
egalitarian and non-authoritarian;   therapy is based on a
loving, accepting relationship being established between a
child and one or more adults.   The emphasis on egalitarian,
non-authoritarian relationships is similar to that in adult
therapeutic communities but does not extend to the allocation
of roles in the community, where adults still exert certain
kinds of traditional authority - e.g. matron arranges bed-
times.   The emphasis on individual adult-child relationships
differs from the emphasis on relationships between residents
in most adult communities.

Wills gave several advantages of the system of shared responsibility over conventional authority, some of which betray
slightly mixed motives - e.g. the fact that adults so seldom
give orders tends to make their authority more effective when
they do.   Other advantages are identical with those which

apply in adult therapeutic communities: it is a natural
vehicle for group therapy, a means by which the children learn
that socially acceptable behaviour is demanded of them not
only as a result of staff prejudice but also by their peers,
and a way of learning that rules exist for the mutual protection of individuals.   Two other features link planned environment therapy and adult therapeutic communities.   One is the
therapeutic value accorded to the work of actually making and
servicing the community.   The second is the use of psychoanalytic concepts, especially in handling the intense relationships between children and staff.

Planned environment therapy, although not synonymous with
the adult democratic therapeutic community, resembles it in
more ways than it differs from it.   Both recognise the emotional healing power and opportunity for social maturation
which can occur when people have jointly to take responsibility for the community they live in.   Both emphasise the
importance of an atmosphere of adult-child (staff-patient)
equality and acceptance, and the need for essentially non-
authoritarian relationships.   The difference lies in the
separation of specifically therapeutic relationships, often
between the child and a particular adult, from the more per-
vasive social learning which takes place in the rest of the
community.   In the adult therapeutic community, where the
need for a substitute parent may be less pressing, these two
aspects of therapy are usually blended together.

In 1966 the Planned Environment Therapy Trust was formed
to promote the study and use of this form of therapy, which
it continues to do through publications and meetings.
Present-day examples include New Barns School at Toddington,
Peper Harow at Godalming, and the Cotswold Community at
Ashton Keynes.

PSYCHIATRY MEETS THE SECOND WORLD WAR: A TALE OF TWO MILITARY
HOSPITALS

Although many of the ingredients of democratic, analytic therapeutic communities were already being used in therapeutic
education, they emerged quite independently in psychiatric
hospitals during the Second World War.   In fact they emerged
in two hospitals at more or less the same time.   One of these
was Northfield military hospital in Birmingham, to which a
number of psychoanalysts and social psychologists were posted
between 1943 and 1946.   The other was a temporarily converted
public school at Mill Hill, near London, where in 1939 a young

research psychiatrist went to take charge of a unit for
patients with psychosomatic anxieties.   His name was Maxwell
Jones.

   Among those who worked at Northfield, three will occupy our
attention as innovators of this new approach in psychiatry.
First, there was W.R. Bion, who later became famous for his
experiential groups at the Tavistock Clinic, and for his
general contributions to psychoanalysis.   Then there was
S.H. Foulkes, who created a method of therapy called group
analysis, and later formed the Institute of Group Analysis.
Third, there was Tom Main, who subsequently became the director of the Cassel Hospital, and who had coined the term 'therapeutic community' to describe what went on at Northfield.
It was, however, Maxwell Jones, working quite independently at
Mill Hill, who was to carry the banner for therapeutic communities after the Second World War and whose name has been most
closely associated with them ever since.   Both hospitals
have an interesting story to tell, but Northfield's is the
more complex.   It is a story that has often been referred to
but seldom told in sufficient detail.

Northfield Hospital

W.R. Bion was posted to Northfield early in 1943, at a time
when unruly conditions in the hospital required someone with
a firm hand.   He was put in charge of what was called the
Training Wing - to which patients were moved after their
initial four weeks in the Hospital Wing and before they were
posted back to the units, or as many hoped, discharged from
active service.   When Bion arrived he found things were disorganised.   Patients were absent without leave, requesting
leave on various pretexts or over-staying the leave they had,
while the officers were uncertain what their duties were supposed to be.   'What was required', he wrote, 'was the sort of
discipline achieved in a theatre of war by an experienced
officer in command of a rather scallywag battalion.   But what
sort of discipline is that?'   He decided to regard discipline
not just as his problem but as a communal problem, to make it
the common enemy to be studied and tackled by the entire
training wing of about 100 men, as they would study an outside
enemy. (4)

   In order to try to bring about such a remarkable shift in
the patients' attitudes he announced a framework of various
activities which he expected the men to take part in.   He
also instituted a daily 'parade' of thirty minutes for the men

to step outside this framework and look at its working.   The
men were free to react as they chose but would have their
behaviour noted.   This freedom he calculated would provide an
opportunity for their true aims to show, while the framework
would provide something against which the unruliness and in-
discipline of individuals could be highlighted and discussed.
He refused, at least outwardly, to have the cure for discipline made his responsibility.   When some of the men complained that others were shirking he attempted to use this as
a starting point for discussion of the problem.   He found
that his determination produced,

> after a vivid and healthy impatience, a real belief that
> the unit was meant to tackle its job with scientific seri-
> ousness ... within a month of the inception of the scheme
> changes had taken place.   Whereas at first it seemed dif-
> ficult to find ways of employing the men, at the end of the
> month it was difficult to find time for the work they
> wanted to do.

Despite its success, the experiment ended after six weeks.
Recounting it some years later Tom Main said, 'Neither the
commanding officer nor his staff was able to tolerate the
early weeks of chaos, and both were condemning and rancorous
about Bion's refusal to own total responsibility for the disorder of others.'   The upshot was that both Bion and the
commanding officer were removed when their rows came to the
notice of higher authority.   Here ended the first lesson
which, according to Main, was that Bion 'had failed to work
at and get and maintain social sanction for his deeds ... he
had been therapeutic for his ward but antitherapeutic for the
military staff.' (5)

Bion left Northfield in May 1943.   He had been there for
three months. (6)   Two months later Foulkes - a psychoanalyst
who was at that time pioneering small group therapy with his
private patients - was appointed as a senior psychiatrist in
charge of one of the wards on the hospital wing.   Clearly the
aftermath of Bion's departure was still around, for although
Foulkes knew nothing of Bion's experiment when he arrived at
Northfield, he found that the training wing (which Bion had
run) was now run by military training officers and the psychiatrists were expected to limit their activities to the
hospital wing.   Foulkes was at Northfield from 1943 till
1946, and was able to chart in detail what he later called the
'second experiment' in creating a therapeutic community - this
time more slowly and more securely sanctioned.   He outlined
four phases: (7)

Phase 1.   The hospital was rigidly divided into different sections with little co-ordination between them or between the medical staff.   It was a forbidding and uncomfortable place, and new patients 'soon found their way, not to their duties but to Jones's cafe nearby'.   In other words it was a typical large institution with two cultures: the official one imposed by the staff, and the unofficial one to which the patients looked for support and information. During this phase Foulkes treated only his own ward patients in groups.

Phase 2.   After a year the administrators appeared to lose some of their suspicion of psychiatrists, who were allowed to continue their involvement with patients when they were transferred to the training wing.   Co-ordination between the medical staff improved, the nurses became more actively involved in decision-making, and barriers between staff throughout the hospital began to lessen.   Foulkes extended his groups, using new techniques such as psychodrama (he knew of Moreno's work) and teaching interested staff and visitors about groups.   As yet patients were not involved in running any hospital activities.

Phase 3.   After about six months came the real beginnings of a therapeutic community.   It coincided with the arrival of several new staff with an interest in group psychology. Among them were Harold Bridger, an enthusiastic exponent of leaderless small groups, and a new lieutenant colonel to whom Foulkes would be responsible, Tom Main.   Both Foulkes and Main saw as their task the furthering of the group treatment of patients.   Aided by Bridger's enthusiasm, not only therapy groups but also patient-organised group projects began to flourish.   The training wing became transformed into an organisation for promoting activities of all sorts.   Hobby groups formed, a newspaper group, a chess group, a drama group, a printing group, a typing group, and so on.   Foulkes described the therapeutic value of this as follows:

> As far as possible the patients' activities were organised and maintained by the patients themselves; if they failed in their responsibility they carried the onus and shared the disability; if the (patient) band did not turn up for the dance there was no dance, but if they succeeded they had their own reward - the result was that above all they became active on their own behalf and used the hospital for their own benefit instead of waiting for good to be done to them.

In contrast with the split cultures in Phase 1 there was now one culture in which the patients and staff were both involved. Patients shared in hospital management, and there was contact between patients, nurses, doctors, and other staff in the meetings and common work in which they were all engaged. The extent of these changes brought their own problems. 'Because the groups contained human beings,' wrote Main, 'troubles abounded, inefficiency, quarrels, arguments, sulks and walkouts occurred.' Foulkes became a kind of troubleshooter, going to wherever a crisis had arisen, to work out with the group what the problem was and how best to resolve it. Yet the final hurdle in the experiment lay not with the patients but with the hospital as a whole.

Phase 4. Morale in the hospital was beginning to sag and spontaneity was diminishing once more. Various causes for this were diagnosed. Foulkes saw it as a problem of what had been new and fresh becoming institutionalised. New patients arriving felt as though the system was imposed on them, just as it had been in Phase 1. The solution he saw was to start off a new round of patient-organised activities which would once more bring everyone into spontaneous and productive contact, to 'get the hospital as a whole again to play as a concerted orchestra.' (7)

Main's solution was on a different level. He identified problems among the staff as the underlying malaise. It has since become a well established part of therapeutic community practice that staff should have regular meetings to discuss difficulties in their relationships, yet the reasons for this are not always appreciated. Much later Main looked back at this period and described how his ideas took shape at that time. I think his account conveys a sense of discovery that makes it worth quoting at length:

Northfield was now, by 1946, a hospital of a new kind, in which both patients and therapeutic staff sought to explore in a way never attempted before the unconscious tensions which pain the lives of individuals and of the small groups they find themselves living in. It looked - as Foulkes teased me - highly chaotic, but both hospital divisions were in fact busy, efficient and relatively free from unresolvable internal tensions. It was also innovative and exciting. Yet in the larger hospital there were strains. Something was not quite right.

In the larger community many of the non-therapeutic

military staff, administrative, domestic, maintenance and
to a lesser extent secretarial, were of low morale. Some
openly resented patients taking the right of action or
decision over matters of work or equipment and it was true
that patients would organise group discussions and activities which regularly overlapped or contradicted or inter-
fered with the military staff's wishes, duties or expectations. The staff were being ignored and after all they,
not the patients, were there to run things. Treatment was
treatment: fair enough; patients should be treated kindly
because they were ill but they should do what they were
told; when things went wrong staff should step in and correct things and show the way; it should not be left to
patients to sort out troubles; things had gone too far;
it was the psychiatrists.

My commanding officer made it plain that his tolerance
was now at an end, and I began to think about Bion's fate.
I had resolved however not to share it, however noble that
would be, and wondered how to preserve the tottering sanctions for our work. I tried not to feel either too guilty
or too righteous and wronged - without great success - and
to free myself to think about my commanding officer's
plight. Why could he not control his staff and support
our work? Why had this otherwise pleasant, intelligent
man become regularly stupid, angry and threatening? Why
did he feel himself threatened by events? With some difficulty I ceased to be so self-centred and began to see
that he had troubles of his own. He was responsible to
his seniors and he was also the inevitable repository for
all the grumbles and discontents of his military, administrative and artisan staff which I and others, safe in our
military rank and medical authority, had ignored or brushed
aside as reactionary. Yet he was being fed by his military juniors with these discontents as the head of the
administrative and domestic hierarchy of the hospital which
was separate and distinct from the therapeutic hierarchy
which I represented.

I then realised that the almost daily rows he and I conducted were about unresolved tensions, not between him and
me as individuals but between the lower-order systems of
military and therapeutic staff fed upwards and into us.
These tensions had been regarded as nuisances, issues not
for open study or scientific scrutiny but for noisy argument or silent power struggles. He and I were being unconsciously required by our own staffs to be their cham-
pions and to conduct these struggles on their behalf; and

we had been unconscious of this.   So now there was a new
set of problems.   How to ensure that the tensions could be
examined, perhaps resolved, where they began - between
people in the lower hospital systems?   How to put the
lower-order military staff in touch with the needs of the
lower-order therapeutic staff and patients?   And vice
versa.   What were the unconscious fantasies each system
grew about the other?   How much blind mutual projection of
evil was going on and distorting perceptions of each other?

One evening I suddenly realised the whole community, all
staff as well as all patients, needed to be viewed as a
troubled larger system which needed treatment.   Could all
people in it move to consideration of other people's
plight, and benefit from opportunities to examine the conscious and unconscious uses each was making of others?
Could the total institution become therapeutic for all?
Clearly we would need a total culture of enquiry if we were
regularly to examine, understand and perhaps resolve the
tensions and defensive use of roles which are inevitable in
any total system.   Today the concept is well-worn, and the
term I coined for it - The Therapeutic Community - is now
in use so widespread that the coinage is somewhat debased;
but then it was new and for me at least it was a sudden insight, a major conceptual shift, a new way of viewing
events in a hospital.   It also demanded appropriate viewing instruments.   At this level of system - a whole community - techniques of investigation and intervention had yet
to be devised;   indeed today argument about them still
seems wholly proper.   But now at Northfield inter-staff
relations and staff-patient relations began to be seen as
legitimate matters for regular, indeed essential, study
whereas hitherto only patient-staff, patient-doctor and
patient interrelations had been.   This attempt to create
an atmosphere of respect for all and the examination of all
difficulties would be a long way from the medical model,
whereby disease is skillfully treated in anonymous people
under blanket medical compassion and served by a clinically
aloof and separate administration. (8)

It may be helpful to summarise the key ideas which were
developed at Northfield by Bion, Foulkes and Main.

1 The problem of disruptive behaviour in the ward is
defined as a shared, common problem rather than the
leader's problem.   Bion identifies it as the 'common
enemy' to be studied and attacked.   (This was a particularly apt metaphor in wartime.)

2   A clear programme of events, activities, etc., is set up
through which patients are free to move as they choose
rather than having it imposed on them.   In this way individuals' true intentions are revealed, to be contrasted
with their professed ones.   Their behaviour and responses
are then reviewed in regular meetings at which attendance
is required.

3   Groups are set up with various tasks which lead the members to have mutual expectations of one another and to com-
municate and co-operate with others.   Foulkes sees the
activity itself as secondary, from a therapeutic point of
view, to the social interactions it fosters.

4   Leadership is used not as an end in itself but as a
stepping stone towards patients taking it over.   Leadership needs first to be securely established by staff and
then given up as patients grow to assume it themselves.

5   A 'culture of inquiry' is established.   This especially
includes the relationships between the staff, whose frustrations are otherwise directed towards heads of department
who get into repetitive conflicts with one another.

6   It is recognised that innovation in one part of an
organisation always affects other parts, and that it is
vital to work with all the affected parts of the organisation if the innovation is not to be attacked by them.

7   The term 'a therapeutic community' is used by Main as a
general label for these new ideas.

Mill Hill Hospital

In contrast to Northfield, there were no special problems of
low morale, unruly behaviour, or conflict amongst the staff
at Mill Hill when Maxwell Jones arrived there in 1940.   Part
of London's Maudsley Hospital had been evacuated there at the
outbreak of war and the unit of which he was in charge had
been set up to study what was known as effort syndrome. (9)
This was a condition in which physical exercise caused people
to become breathless and giddy, and to suffer from palpita-
tions and chest pains.   Such patients were often convinced
that they had a serious heart disease.   This was a prevalent
condition in wartime and during the six years he was there
over 2,000 patients passed through the unit.

At this stage in his career Jones was primarily interested
in physiological research, and had only a passing and sceptical interest in psychoanalysis.   For the first two years he
conducted numerous experiments designed to determine the precise nature and causes of effort syndrome.   He was a good
researcher, and his thesis describing this work won him a gold
medal from Edinburgh University.   He was also an openminded
and practical scientist.   Having determined the physiological
mechanisms which underlay effort syndrome, he reasoned that if
these patients could understand for themselves how their symptoms were caused, they might stop worrying about their hearts.
His aim was not to cure them but to change their attitudes, to
enable them to recognise that they had a minor disability
rather than a major illness.

In 1941 he decided to introduce a series of lectures to
educate the patients about human physiology.   Three times a
week 100 men gathered to listen and discuss their symptoms.
Then an unexpected thing began to happen.   Patients who had
already completed the 'course' of lectures and had not yet
left the hospital began to help by explaining things to the
newcomers, and became enthusiastic and unexpectedly articulate
in doing so.

Jones was not slow to recognise the beneficial effects of
patients helping one another in this way;   it brought out
what was 'well' and healthy in them, increasing morale and
self-esteem.   From this beginning the unit gradually moved
towards patients taking a more equal role with the staff in
other activities.   This was helped by the fact that the
nurses were mostly conscripts who, lacking traditional training in nurse-patient relationships, were happy to change
towards a more democratic way of working.

As this approach evolved over the next four years, so its
application widened beyond changing the attitude of patients
towards their symptoms.   Later Jones wrote that it soon
became apparent that the patients' reactions in the hospital
'were similar to their reactions outside, and the study of
these real life situations (in the hospital) gave a great
deal of information about the patient's problems.'   It was
in order to make the most use of this new approach that he
evolved a new hospital structure which included 'more open
communication;   less rigid hierarchy of doctors, nurses,
patients;   daily structured discussions of the whole unit,
and various subgroups.' (9)

Thus Jones evolved an approach which began to look increas-

ingly like the one at Northfield.   Although less dramatic
than events at that hospital, developments at Mill Hill were
in their own way just as remarkable, perhaps even more so
given Jones's lack of prior acquaintance with group techniques.   The convergence of psychiatrists with quite different backgrounds - psychoanalysis and physiological research -
on the idea of using the way a hospital was run as the basis
of therapy was a sign that a basic shift in psychiatric thinking was in the making.   Psychiatry had met the Second World
War and made creative use of the encounter.

Chapter 4
From innovation to application

MAXWELL JONES AND THE HENDERSON HOSPITAL

Although it was Tom Main who coined the term 'a therapeutic
community', it was Maxwell Jones whose name came to symbolise
the movement that was to occupy a significant place in western
psychiatry in the years after the war. Today the ideas and
methods which most psychiatric staff refer to when they speak
of a therapeutic community are those developed by Maxwell
Jones, his colleagues and successors, at the unit which since
1958 has been called Henderson Hospital, or simply the
Henderson. (1)

After the war Jones wanted to continue his interest in the
way hospitals were organised, and his clinical interest shif-
ted from patients with psychosomatic symptoms to those whose
problems were primarily social and interpersonal. For a year
he ran a transitional community, rehabilitating emotionally
disturbed prisoners-of-war returning to Britain after many
years in prison camps. In 1947 he became the director of a
new unit set up to tackle the problem of unemployed 'drifters',
at Belmont hospital in Surrey. Initially this was called the
Industrial Neurosis Unit, later the Social Rehabilitation
Unit, and in 1958 coinciding with Jones's own departure to
America it was renamed Henderson Hospital. It was and remains probably the best-known psychiatric therapeutic community, specialising in the treatment of psychopaths. At Belmont Jones and his colleagues developed a number of procedures
and principles which could be readily applied by others. If
Bion, Foulkes and Main had created a feast of new ideas at
Northfield, it was Jones who sat down and produced the recipe
that others could follow. Three of the key ingredients were
'community meetings', 'staff review meetings', and 'living-
learning situations'.

At a daily 'community meeting' all the staff and patients meet in a large circle to discuss what has been going on in the community over the past twenty-four hours and to examine any problems that have come up.   This is the focus or hub of the community, into which events in other group meetings and activities are 'fed back', and in which decisions and ideas are debated, with the staff not necessarily taking a leading role.   Such meetings can have various aims, as discussed in Chapter 1.   For Jones, two aims were central.   Taking a responsible part in the affairs of the community helped patients to overcome their lack of confidence and low self-esteem, and through discussion of particular incidents patients could learn what feelings and perceptions lie behind behaviour, testing distorted perceptions against the common consensus.

Immediately following each community meeting there is a 'staff review meeting' in which the interactions in the community meeting are discussed.   This is particularly useful for training new staff and examining the relationships between staff.   Many staff have been trained in traditional hospitals, and the change from traditional staff roles can give rise to considerable anxiety and frustration.   The overlap of responsibilities between doctors and nurses and between staff and patients mean that clarification is continually needed concerning who takes responsibility for what. To take an example, in a traditional ward everyone considers it the nurses' responsibility to see that the ward is kept clean and tidy.   In a therapeutic community this is often regarded as the patients' responsibility.   Nurses new to this method who find this difficult to accept may need to discuss their feelings about this change in their role. Similarly doctors, used to being the main decision-makers, may find it hard to share decisions with the rest of the staff and the patients.   The staff review session provides an opportunity for newcomers to learn and for all staff to sort out problems inherent in the relationships between different disciplines.

One of the terms Jones is best known for is the 'living-learning situation'.   Today the term 'crisis intervention' has a similar meaning.   The 'real life' nature of a therapeutic community means that from time to time crises occur involving all or some of the members of the community. Rather than wait for the next community meeting, a meeting is immediately called of all the people concerned in the crisis. Jones describes this as a

face to face confrontation and joint analysis of the current interpersonal difficulty.   Each individual is helped
to become more aware of the thinking and the feeling of
the others and this leads to a more comprehensive view of
the situation as it affects each of the people involved.
... Frequent exposure to situations of this kind if handled
skilfully can contribute to personal growth and maturation. (1)

Other ingredients evolved by Jones and the Henderson staff
include work groups followed by discussion between the members about their responses during the work; role-play of
situations outside hospital which residents may have to face;
and a selection committee for new patients which is made up
of staff and residents in equal proportion, with equal voting
rights.

In addition a wide range of posts were created to which
residents could be elected, e.g. work co-ordinator, ward representative, chairman, etc.   There are also two terms which
have entered into the daily vocabulary of psychiatry - role-
blurring and feedback.   'Role-blurring' is itself a rather
blurred term.   It was originally used to refer to the overlap or flexibility of roles which occurred in therapeutic
communities, where a nurse could do a job normally carried
out by a social worker, or a doctor could do something normally done by a nurse, and so on.   This could naturally
create some confusion without frequent staff discussions,
and today role-blurring is often used to refer to the situation where roles are not properly defined and people are uncertain about their role.   Role-blurring need not lead to
role confusion if sufficient discussion takes place about who
is doing what.

'Feedback' usually refers to the practice of reporting
back in a meeting something of therapeutic importance that
happened elsewhere.   A conversation between two people may
be 'fed back' to a group, or events in small group meetings
may be 'fed back' into the community meeting.   This is done
in the belief that community members are in the best position
to understand and help one another if they are fully informed
about each other's feelings and behaviour.   This may appear
to breach the ethics of confidentiality, but since it is the
community as a whole that 'treats' the patient rather than
the doctor, the principle of confidentiality now extends to
the whole community.   In practice this may be difficult for
some newcomers to accept, and the amount of detail contained
in a feedback may need to be modified according to the level
of trust which has been built up between community members.

In addition to Jones's own work, in the 1950s he invited a
team of sociologists led by Robert Rapoport to study the
Social Rehabilitation Unit (as it was then called).   The
result was an important book, 'Community as Doctor', published
in 1960.   Among the team's findings was the occurrence of a
repeated cycle of oscillations within the community.   At certain times residents were able to take a lot of responsibility
and the unit ran quite democratically.   There then occurred a
series of disturbances which escalated to the point where the
staff played a more active role for a while, until residents
once more became involved in the running of the community.
The account of these oscillations has been of great relevance
to other communities where similar cycles have been noticed.
The book also highlighted a conflict between those staff who
were mainly interested in preparing residents for the outside
world, and those who focused on what was going on within the
community and on helping residents to understand themselves
better.   This was conceptualised as a conflict between the
goals of rehabilitation and treatment.   Again this has been
found in many other communities.

The most widely known finding in Rapoport's work was the
result of a questionnaire dealing with the values that the
staff held about treatment.   Four principles emerged which
have since become synonymous with therapeutic communities of
the democratic analytic type.

1 'Democratisation': every member of the community (i.e.
all patients and staff) should share equally in the exercise of power in decision-making about community affairs.

2 'Permissiveness': all members should tolerate from one
another a wide degree of behaviour that might be distressing or seem deviant by ordinary standards.

3 'Communalism': there should be tight-knit, intimate
sets of relationships, with sharing of amenities (dining
room, etc.), use of first names, and free communication.

4 'Reality-confrontation': patients should be continuous-
ly presented with interpretations of their behaviour as it
is seen by others, in order to counteract their tendency to
distort, deny or withdraw from their difficulties in getting on with others.

There is some discrepancy between these values, shared by
the staff, and Maxwell Jones's own views.   For example he saw
democracy as giving residents 'that degree of responsibility

which is compatible with their capacity at any one time'.
The difference between this and the 'equal exercise of power'
is the difference between seeing the therapeutic community as
a method of treatment to be used at the discretion of the
therapist, and seeing it as an ideology concerned with the
abolition of inequality between different classes - in this
case residents and staff.   The practical consequences of
these two views may often be the same, when the community is
in the democratic phase of its oscillations.   At other times
disagreements may develop between those who see democracy in
ideological or therapeutic terms.

It is useful to realise that the principles of permissiveness and reality-confrontation go together: patients can do
what they like but whatever they do will be a matter for confrontation and discussion if it interferes with their relationships with others.   This combination of permissiveness
with confrontation and interpretation is central to all therapies based directly or indirectly on psychoanalysis.   It
links the Henderson with Bion's attempt to get his men to
study their own disorderly behaviour, and with the refusal of
the pioneer educationalists to impose adult authority on maladjusted children.

Today the Henderson hospital continues to function as a
therapeutic community of the democratic analytic type, and
also as a centre for visits and training courses.

TOM MAIN AND THE CASSEL HOSPITAL

The Henderson has provided the model of a therapeutic community most often referred to in psychiatry, but there are
others.   One is the Cassel Hospital, which began as a small,
private hospital for neurotic disorders in 1919 and gradually
developed a psychoanalytic orientation.   In 1946 Tom Main
moved from Northfield to become its new director, a post which
he held for over thirty years.   In 1948 this was the only
psychiatric hospital in the new National Health Service where
all the doctors were trained or training in psychoanalysis.
It might have continued simply as a psychotherapy hospital for
neurosis but under Main's influence there evolved a unique
system, combining a therapeutic community in which nurses and
patients participated as equals, with individual or group psychotherapy which took place between the patients and the doctors.   In effect there was a quite deliberate separation
between the 'outer' world of social roles, work tasks and
current relationships, and the 'inner' world of private

fantasy and feelings. Here the conflict between the goals of treatment and rehabilitation which had troubled the Henderson staff was resolved by creating two parallel systems of therapy.

The role of the nurse was of particular interest. It was considered important that she should be regarded not as a second-rate psychotherapist but as a professional with a role distinct from the doctor's. This role was given the name 'psychosocial nursing'. The Cassel became a major centre for postgraduate training of nurses in this specialised type of work and produced a book about it. (2) In psychosocial nursing the main task is to help the community and its members to 'get on with the work and maintain adult roles'. Nurses work with the patients rather than for them, as equal, responsible citizens (the same term that Homer Lane used to describe the members of the Little Commonwealth). 'Each group, with an elected manager, is responsible for maintaining, cleaning and decorating a particular area of the hospital, and for managing its own work programme.' The nurse may help the members to learn from their behaviour, but prevents the group becoming preoccupied with therapeutic problems that distract from the tasks in hand.

This division of the doctors' and the nurses' roles contrasts with the principle of role-blurring between staff, and of blending practical and therapeutic tasks, which is characteristic of most therapeutic communities described in this chapter. It presents an interesting use of therapeutic community democracy within an overall structure in which staff take specialised therapeutic roles. Although this may seem, from an ideological point of view, to be opposed to the therapeutic community ethic, from a therapeutic point of view such a structure may be seen as a way of helping psychologically disorganised patients to gain a sense of control over their feelings and experience. External structure provides a model for internal order. It is an approach similar to the one used by some pioneers of therapeutic education, and also resembles that of the concept-based therapeutic communities to be described later.

WIDER APPLICATIONS

Therapeutic communities based on the principles of democratic participation and psychoanalytic understanding were first tried in schools for maladjusted children, and later developed in psychiatric hospitals specialising in the treatment of

neurotic or psychopathic disorders.   The principles and
methods worked out in these places have subsequently been
taken up, modified, and applied in a wide range of treatment
settings.

In America, Australia and many European countries, therapeutic communities have been created in small units for particular disorders and in general psychiatric hospitals.   The
principles have also been applied outside psychiatric hospitals - in prisons, hostels and day centres.   The extent of
these developments has probably been related to the prevailing attitudes in different countries and in different professions.   Therapeutic communities are more likely to be established where there is a certain liberalisation in progress in
the political climate, and where there is a questioning of
conventional forms of medical and social work practice. (3)

The following short accounts are based on my own acquaintance with particular projects, either at first hand or
through books and articles.   They indicate the sorts of
things which are possible, and are not necessarily a representative cross-section of the way therapeutic community
principles have been applied.

Prisons

A prison might be the last place you would expect to find a
therapeutic community.   Prisons have traditionally been for
taking away people's freedom, imposing rigid discipline and
limiting their opportunity for social involvement.   Yet
there have been some experiments aimed at making prisons
therapeutic.   Some of these were limited to the introduction
of individual or group counselling, or to improving the environment and relaxing the formality.   In the 1960s two
attempts were made to run part or all of a prison as a therapeutic community on the lines of the Henderson: one at Chino
in California, the other at Grendon Underwood in Buckingham-
shire, England.

At Chino a project was undertaken by Dennie Briggs, a clinical psychologist, to create a therapeutic community for fifty
of the prisoners, who volunteered for the project.   An
initial year was allowed for training staff, working out group
procedures and starting, with a small group of enthusiastic
volunteers, to create a 'culture' that would influence the
main group when they came.   The programme included regular
community meetings, small psychotherapy groups and work

groups.   There was a good deal of apprehensiveness to begin
with.

    We needed to know how convicted felons in prison would take
    to a culture which required 'feedback' to operate.   Would
    they see this as 'snitching'?   Would they be able to vio-
    late the well established 'inmate code of ethics' and feed
    incidences of delinquent behaviour publicly into the meet-
    ings?   If men were encouraged to talk openly about their
    current anxieties at being in prison, would their feelings
    erupt and get out of control?   Could you contain anger and
    hostility in large groups?   What would happen to staff
    control if inmates talked too freely?

    Early large group meetings were viewed with consider-
    able anxiety by the custodial officials.   The first meet-
    ing with over twenty men was a cautious experience.   Extra
    custodial officials were stationed nearby in case anger
    erupted and became unmanageable. (4)

No ill-effects resulted, and the staff and inmates began to
relax.   Despite this, prison officers were reluctant to
become involved in the discussions as they believed that open
confrontation would jeopardise their authority.   Particular
problems arose over the work arrangements in the prison
laundry.   This serviced the whole prison and a number of
'rackets' were being operated there, common to institutions
with an active 'underlife', which clashed with the values of
the project.   There was also the same kind of conflict as Tom
Main had described at Northfield, between the custodial and
therapeutic staff.   The former expected delinquent behaviour,
if found out, to be punished, while the latter were against
taking disciplinary action.

    As more delinquent activities were reported and no action
    taken, custodial officials in the institution became more
    alarmed and viewed the project as a place fostering delin-
    quency rather than controlling it.... Some of the policy
    makers, as a result of brief visits, became concerned that
    the inmates had been given too much freedom.

The future of the project seemed at risk, when a more serious
crisis involving the whole prison proved to be its salvation.
An incident between a white member of the project and a black
inmate not in the project had created an explosive situation
which seemed destined to escalate into a race riot.   Prisoners and staff were both amassing weapons in readiness.   A
crisis meeting of staff and inmates was called in the thera-

peutic community and an open sharing of staff frustration led
to an effort to work together to avert the riot.   The anticipated riot did not take place and the project at last won the
confidence of the prison authorities.

Developments at Grendon Underwood were different since the
whole prison was designed to function as a collection of wings
each run as a separate therapeutic community.   It was built
as a unique experiment within the English prison system and
remains the only one of its kind, although smaller therapeutic
communities have been set up at Wormwood Scrubs and in the
Special Unit at Barlinnie prison in Glasgow.   As at Chino,
attention was paid at Grendon to establishing the right atmosphere.   Care was taken to avoid creating a prison sub-culture
by taking men, who all came from other prisons, only a few at
a time.   A total of about 200 prisoners were to be catered
for, most of them in their teens and twenties, within a year
or so from their release.

One of the main effects of running the prison as a therapeutic community was to break down the traditional roles which
prisoners and officers created for themselves and each other -
enshrined in the terms 'cons' and 'screws'.   Prisoners were
able to give up the need to impress their peers.   One said,

'Here you have the freedom to drop any fronts, to be yourself.   You don't have to live a lie.   You don't have to
pretend to a bigtime gangster.   Here I can say I'm a petty
thief.   And sex cases don't have to cower in the corner.'

The effect could be as marked for officers as for inmates, as
it was for one tough disciplinarian who was transferred to
Grendon against his wishes.   He was wholly out of sympathy
with the system, and refused to attend wing meetings on the
grounds that he had no wish to hear what inmates had to say.
Over a period of time his attitude changed.   Asked to describe what happened, he said, 'At X (the prison he'd come
from) they were all cons.   Here they're blokes.'

In the 1970s a major study was undertaken to evaluate what
effects Grendon had.   It was found that inmates left feeling
less anxious and depressed, more self-confident, better able
to relate to people and less hostile towards society.   The
study was unable to find a properly matched group of prisoners
to compare for rates of reconviction, but suggested that there
was no difference in this respect between Grendon and other
prisons. (5)

Acute psychiatric units

Therapeutic communities of the democratic analytic type were
not originally intended for acutely disturbed, psychotic
patients. Such patients are usually treated in the admission
wards of general psychiatric hospitals, where treatment often
consists of medication and electroconvulsive therapy (ECT),
with the use of physical restraint or seclusion if patients
become violent. As in general hospitals patients are often
kept in bed or wander round in dressing gowns. Their day
is largely unstructured apart from individual interviews with
the doctor. In the better wards there may be recreational
facilities and occupational therapy. Since the 1950s a small
number of psychiatrists in Britain and America were sufficiently influenced by therapeutic community ideas, and in particular by Maxwell Jones's work, to attempt to run their acute
wards on therapeutic community lines. How they actually did
this varied considerably, from simply holding a daily community meeting to creating a highly organised environment with
an elaborate system of patient roles and group activities.

In most cases these units continued to use drugs and ECT
to treat the biochemical aspect of the patient's disturbance,
but physical restraint and seclusion were used much less, if
at all. Talking about outbursts of aggressive behaviour in
meetings enabled many crises to be contained. Generally the
staff retained responsibility for decisions affecting treatment, although problems and requests concerning medication or
discharge could be discussed openly between patients and
staff. The staff also had to be active in creating and
maintaining the community norms since patients' stayed a
relatively short time - often only a matter of weeks.

The goals of treatment in these units are in part the same
as those in any admission unit - to reduce the patient's level
of overt disturbance so that he can return home as soon as
possible. Added to this is often the goal that the patient
will learn to behave in an acceptable way and will not make
use of his illness as an excuse for antisocial behaviour
which is in fact within his control. This is a goal which
requires delicate judgment, since a too strident insistence
on normal behaviour may overlook the reality, to the patient,
of his difficulties; yet undoubtedly the expectations of
those around him will affect his behaviour. Another aspect
of a therapeutic community admission ward is that it can enhance the overall running of the unit. Daily meetings ensure
that all patients are regularly seen and taken account of, the
relative absence of formality and hierarchy helps to create

good staff relationships and ensure that support is readily
available at times of crisis, and the overall group morale is
one that enhances the effect of more specific treatments.
All this is not to underplay the particular difficulties of
this application of therapeutic community ideas.   The fast
rate of turnover among patients and the highly disturbed state
of some patients on admission can mean frequent disruptions to
the daily programme and rapid changes in the level of responsibility which patients are able to take.   One week patients
may be organising an outing, the next they may be angrily
demanding that the staff take charge of everything.   Such
work is seldom dull and often frustrating.

One way to cope with these fluctuations is to have a
highly structured system of roles and expectations into which
the new patient is introduced - emphasising from the start the
expectation of 'normal' behaviour.   (The feasibility of this
approach may depend on whether there is somewhere else to send
patients who are too disruptive to fit into it.)   An example
of this type of unit was Tomkins I which was opened in 1960 in
the Yale-New Haven Community hospital and has been extensively
studied and written about.   A number of specific roles were
introduced for patients to help them take responsibility for
one another.   These included a patients Advisory Board which
decided which patients were ready for passes to leave the
ward,   a 'buddy system' which enabled new patients to go off
the ward if accompanied by another who had a pass, and Psychiatric Trustees who took responsibility for more disturbed
patients.   Suggestions for some of these roles came initially
from the patients and were then incorporated into the unit's
routine. (6)

A more recent example has been described in Street Ward in
Fulbourn hospital, Cambridge.   Here new patients are met by
the duty nurse and by the 'duty resident', a patient elected
for the week, who give them a tour of the unit.   A booklet
explains how the community works and gives practical information such as maps and bus timetables.   In addition to the
community meetings, specific meetings are held to cater for
different needs, including group therapy, the day-to-day
affairs of washing-up rotas, etc., and patients' requests
regarding their treatment. (7)

A therapeutic community admission unit may also be run in a
less elaborately structured way, with less emphasis on formal
roles and group tasks, and more on the general quality of support for patients and staff.   This is the approach which has
evolved in the Phoenix Unit at Littlemore hospital in

Oxford. (8)   Here daily community meetings and small groups
provide a framework within which staff encourage patients to
participate at whichever level they are able.   Expectation of
patients taking an active role in the unit are not pre-deter-
mined and depend on individuals' capabilities and motivation.
Activities such as cooking, art and psychodrama are optional.
A consistent emphasis is on staff meetings, and in particular
a weekly unstructured meeting of the whole staff which may
number around thirty (including students from several disciplines).   Here problems of integrating new staff, supporting
those who feel under pressure, sharing anxieties about particular patients, and keeping everyone aware of the tensions inevitable in large groups are among the issues which regularly
come up for discussion.

Patients in admission units are necessarily unselected for
any particular form of treatment, so that the programme of
treatment, whether therapeutic community or not, must be flex-
ible enough to incorporate people with very different problems
and needs.   Units specifically for young schizophrenics have
also been run as therapeutic communities.   At Chestnut Lodge
in Maryland, USA, a small therapeutic community was created in
which ample nursing and medical staff made it possible to deal
with even severe management problems by psychosocial means
rather than medication. (9)   Two other units for young
schizophrenics, Soteria in the United States and Villa 21 in
England, are described in Chapter 6.

Hostels and half-way houses

The term half-way house is usually used to describe a residential hostel set up to provide a stepping stone for psychiatric
patients who have left hospital but are not ready to live
independently in the outside community.   Hostels also exist
for young offenders, alcoholics, the homeless, drug abusers,
and other groups of people in need of residential support.
Hostels are run by a number of statutory bodies in the fields
of health, social service and criminal justice, and by many
independent charitable organisations.   The ways of running
them take in the whole spectrum from highly authoritarian
establishments to very permissive, egalitarian ones.

The most widespread application of therapeutic community
principles in half-way houses is probably that developed by the
Richmond Fellowship.   This has over thirty houses in Great
Britain, several in the United States and Australia, and is
extending its work in other countries.   The Fellowship is the

creation of Elly Jansen, who as a Dutch theology student in
London set up a hostel in 1959 for ex-psychiatric patients.
Its success led to the setting up of a second hostel with
staff and residents from the first. As the Fellowship ex-
panded, its houses began to specialise in particular types of
client - e.g. adults, adolescents, families, drug abusers.
In 1970 Jansen wrote, 'While each house differs according to
its purpose and the personality of staff and residents, the
basic structure has been found applicable to all.'

This structure includes residents organising and doing the
household chores from 9-11 a.m. every morning (apart from
those who have outside jobs), obligatory attendance of all
residents and staff at a weekly community meeting, weekly
individual and group therapy sessions for each resident, and
participation in various work projects. Each member of staff
performs both administrative and therapeutic tasks, as a way
of trying to avoid a split between these two aspects of staff-
resident relationships. The size of the staff team in each
house is small by hospital standards - four or five is typical - with between twelve and twenty residents.

An organisation the size of the Richmond Fellowship presents unusual advantages and problems for its therapeutic
communities. Individual houses benefit from the organisation's support and resources. The Fellowship is large
enough to support newly established houses, and to provide
its own career structure, with a two-year in-service training. On the other hand, the problems of any large organisation are present. Staff in individual houses can feel they
are being required to fit into a mould with little freedom to
experiment, while headquarters staff can feel that house
staff do not appreciate the needs of the overall organisation. Through its system of training and supervision the
Richmond Fellowship manages to sustain a viable balance
between individual initiative and organisational policy. (10)

Day hospitals and day centres

Communities are places where people live and, by and large,
therapeutic communities are too. However, the methods of
the therapeutic community can be applied in day-care settings,
provided enough time is spent together and enough activities
are shared to create a sense of community. This usually
means five days a week, for all or at least half the day.

The first day hospital for psychiatric patients was the

Marlborough Day Hospital in London, set up by Joshua Bierer in
1946. This was part of a comprehensive scheme for helping
patients to be independent of full-time hospital treatment.
This hospital later evolved into a sophisticated therapeutic
community using a wide variety of different group therapy
techniques and considerable involvement of patients in the way
the community was organised. A combination of staff difficulties and external pressures led to the closure of the Marlborough Day Hospital in 1978. (11)

In recent years there has been a trend towards reducing the
length of time patients stay in psychiatric hospitals, and
avoiding admission altogether where possible. This had led
to an increase in the use of day hospitals and day centres.
In many cases these are run on fairly traditional lines,
offering mainly social support and recreational activities.
However, some day centres offer more intensive group psychotherapy, and there is an increasing trend towards involving
patients in the day-to-day running of the centres - e.g.
making rules, selecting new members - in other words towards
creating the culture of a therapeutic community. A pioneering venture of this kind has been St Luke's Project which was
started in Chelsea, London in 1974 'to break the cycle of readmission'. Today the project includes a number of therapeutic community day centres in the same neighbourhood, each
designed for clients with different needs and capabilities. (12)

The Association of Therapeutic Communities

In 1970 the staff of some British hospital-based therapeutic
communities began to hold regular meetings at each other's
communities, for mutual support and to exchange ideas. In
1972 this led to the forming of the Association of Therapeutic Communities. In the past ten years its members have extended to include those from all types of application described in this chapter. Today the Association continues to hold
regular one-day conferences hosted by different communities,
and in addition organises various training activities and pub-
lishes a newsletter and the quarterly 'International Journal
of Therapeutic Communities'. Similar associations have developed in other countries, notably the VWPG in the Netherlands
(see Information section for details).

Chapter 5
Synanon and the concept-based therapeutic community

THE STORY OF SYNANON

The therapeutic communities described in the last three chapters have one important thing in common. They were created
by people like doctors, teachers, and social workers working
in places like hospitals, schools, hostels, prisons, and so
on. In other words, by qualified staff working within the
established framework of care-giving professions and institutions.

In 1958 a quite new kind of therapeutic community was created by a group of ex-alcoholics and drug addicts. It was
called Synanon, and it was the first of what have come to be
known as concept-based therapeutic communities. This name
refers to their adherence to a set of explicit concepts
about the nature of drug addiction and its treatment. Communities of this type have since been established in Europe,
South Africa, Australia and the Far East as well as throughout their native United States.

The inspiration behind Synanon and its successors was provided by an ex-alcoholic called Chuck Dederich. A former
oil company executive, in 1958 Dederich was unemployed and
living in Ocean Park, a 'slum' district in California. He
began holding a weekly discussion group in his apartment,
inviting friends from Alcoholics Anonymous, of which he was
at that time still a member, to participate. Dederich described these as 'free-association' meetings with no particular agenda, although many of the participants had a psychoanalytic orientation. The sociologist Lewis Yablonsky
quotes him as saying: (1)

The meetings were loud and boisterous. Attack of one

64

another was a keynote of the sessions, with everyone joining in.   I could detect considerable lying and self-
deception in the group.   I began to attack viciously -
partly out of my own irritations and at times to defend
myself.   The group would join in, and we would let the
air out of pompously inflated egos, including my own.
The sessions soon became the high point in everybody's
week.

The meetings increased to three nights a week, and more
people began attending - at this stage still mostly ex-alcoholics.   The members decided to rent a building as a 'club-
house' where they could meet during the day.   Already it was
becoming apparent that some were being helped to reduce their
intake of alcohol or drugs.   Soon members began bringing
their friends, who included one or two long-term drug addicts
trying to 'kick' the habit.   Dederich told one of them, an
'incorrigible addict' called Jesse, that if he wanted to succeed he would have to move in and live there.   Jesse stayed,
and stayed off drugs.   It was then, Dederich later said,
that he realised he had a new career.

At this stage, Synanon included both ex-addicts and alcoholics.   The two groups did not get on well together and a
rift soon occurred with the local branch of AA.   From that
time on Synanon was concerned primarily with the rehabilitation of former drug addicts.   The way Synanon got its name
provides an interesting reflection of its aim to help its
members improve their general education.   In addition to the
'attack' groups Dederich had initiated educational seminars
with readings from the works of Freud and religious and philosophical writers.   A newly arrived ex-addict, unfamiliar
with words like symposium and seminar, had stammered out the
request to go to 'another of those sym ... sem ... synanons'.

Having realised that he had a career, Dederich got things
organised.   Using his knowledge of business, he registered
the club as a non-profit making organisation, called The
Synanon Foundation.   He also began to formulate his ideas
about the way it worked, and when a group of parole officers
who were impressed by Synanon's early success invited
Dederich to give a talk, he gave a speech that included the
following statement:

We have here a climate consisting of a family structure
similar in some areas to a primitive tribal structure,
which ... also contains overtones of a nineteenth-century
family of the type which produced inner-directed personal-

ities.   A more or less autocratic family structure
appears to be necessary to buy some time for the recover-
ing addict.   This time is then used to administer doses
of an inner-directed philosophy such as that oulined in
Emerson's essay entitled Self Reliance.   If it seems
paradoxical that an authoritative environment tends to
produce inner direction, it must be remembered that the
inner directed men of the nineteenth century were products
of an authoritative family structure.*

We can see here the importance, early in the development
of concept-based communities, of the model of an autocratic
family with (not stated but implied) the director as its
head.   The assumption that this would create inner-directed
personalities was probably incorrect, for Synanon also created an openness and intimacy which would not have been found
in the kind of families Dederich was thinking of.   Nevertheless it indicates the importance attached to philosophical
and moral values - which later became the 'concepts'.

It is interesting that Dederich refers to 'doses' of philosophy as if it were medicine.   Although in fact offering a
powerful alternative to medical treatment, it is possible
that addressing a professional audience he wanted to use an
image that would be readily understood.   It is also possible
that at this stage Synanon was eager to be accepted as a
legitimate alternative to professional treatment.   Later on
relations with the outside world, and professionals in particular, were to become less friendly.

During 1959 a daily routine took shape at Synanon that was
to form the model for all future concept-based communities.
It included daily job assignments, regular 'synanons' (the
term referred to the attack therapy groups as well as the
organisation as a whole), and daily discussions around philosophical readings.   During this year there was a shift from
residents still using small amounts of drugs to staying completely 'clean' - i.e. drug free.   Already the importance of
'role models' was emerging.   These were former addicts who
had succeeded in giving up drugs, to whom new arrivals could

* The term 'inner-directed' was coined by sociologist David
Riesman, who described three types of personality associated
with three types of society: tradition-directed, inner-
directed and other-directed.   Inner-directed people are
influenced not by what other people say or do but by their
own inner values and convictions.

look as examples to follow.   This fitted in with the idea of
a family in which these 'models' were like older brothers or
sisters.

A year and a half after its first beginnings, Synanon, now
with fifty residents, moved to new premises in Santa Monica,
a well-to-do Los Angeles suburb.   The arrival of this mixed
group of blacks and whites, many with criminal records, in a
smart white residential area, was greeted with predictable
hostility by the local inhabitants.   They tried to get
Synanon moved, on the grounds that it was really a hospital
and was infringing certain 'zoning' regulations.   Official
reports and court hearings followed and at one stage Dederich
was actually imprisoned for a brief period for infringing
'zoning' regulations.   Eventually State and Federal commit-
tees were called on to assess Synanon.   They made reports in
its favour, seeing it as 'a most promising effort to rehabilitate narcotic addicts'.   After a three-year public battle
Synanon was officially approved, and it developed rapidly
into a large organisation, spawning several new communities
and inspiring many copies.

In California and Nevada (a neighbouring state), new communities were set up.   Ex-addicts were invited to run
Synanon groups for addicts in prison, sometimes where they
themselves had been former inmates.   However, the largest
problem of addiction in America was in New York, and it was
there that the major derivatives of Synanon developed.   The
first, Daytop Village, was started in 1963 by a team of psychiatrists and probation officers who had been impressed by a
visit to Synanon.   In its first year the project did not go
well, and the organisers appointed a graduate of Synanon to
take over as director.   He immediately changed Daytop from a
loosely regulated 'half-way house' tolerating illicit drug
use, to a tightly run therapeutic community with the same
rules and values as Synanon.   After three years as a successful Synanon-style community a major conflict developed
between the ex-addict director and the board of management,
which included psychiatrists and members of the church, over
who was in control.   The director left taking many of the
staff and residents with him.   Dan Casriel, a psychiatrist
who had been a member of the team which started Daytop, took
over as director and the community re-established itself.
But conflict between professional and ex-addict staff has
continued to be an emotive issue in concept-based therapeutic
communities. (2)

In 1968 another major organisation was launched: Phoenix

House, New York. Started with the help of Daytop and initially staffed by former Synanon residents, it became the
largest and best-known concept house, with places for about
400 residents at any one time. In 1970 three graduates from
Phoenix House came to Britain to start a community in London,
and in subsequent years concept-based communities were set up
in Oxford, Portsmouth and Dublin. During this period communities were also started in many European countries, notably
Holland, Sweden and West Germany.

The spread of therapeutic communities for ex-drug addicts
is now worldwide, extending to over 30 countries. In the
mid 1970s the International Council on Alcoholism and Addiction gave recognition to this movement and formed a therapeutic communities section. Since 1976 this section has organised an annual World Conference of Therapeutic Communities -
a slightly misleading title in that its main concern is with
drug addiction rather than the whole range of problems
treated in different types of therapeutic communities. In
1980 the World Federation of Therapeutic Communities was
formed, devoted to working with and influencing governments
in planning how the problems of addiction should be tackled
at a national and international level.

During the early 1970s Synanon itself changed its character from a therapeutic community, with the goal of returning
ex-addicts to society as productive citizens, to a permanent
alternative way of life. Synanon City, as it now called
itself, attracted a large number of 'straights' (non-addicts)
as well as former addicts, who came to live there because
they preferred its values and life style to those of society
at large. As Synanon became more inward looking, Dederich
increasingly became a dictator whom no one could challenge.
In 1975 Synanon proclaimed itself a religion, with an aggressive policy towards any opposition. Things came to a head
in 1978 when Dederich and others were arrested on a charge of
conspiracy. They had attempted to harm a lawyer involved
in a legal action brought against Synanon by some relatives
of people who had gone to live there. It was the disastrous
collapse of a career which had spanned twenty years and given
rise to a flourishing worldwide network of therapeutic communities.

The story of Synanon is difficult to be impartial about.
From one point of view - its creators and supporters - it was
a uniquely successful attempt to create an effective form of
self-help for otherwise hopeless drug addicts. From another
point of view - some professionals and some relatives of

those attracted to Synanon - it was a cult which brainwashed
its members into total acceptance of its values and life
style.   The truth is difficult to disentangle; both views
contain some of it.   Any powerful belief system can be both
salvation and entrapment.   Which view you take depends
partly on whether you agree with the particular beliefs and
also on how those who lead such a movement use or misuse
their power.   We will return to consider some of these
issues later in the chapter.

An informed opinion about concept-based therapeutic communities requires an understanding of what they are trying to
do: how they view the problem of drug addiction and how they
set about tackling it.   We will consider this under two
headings, the concepts, and the structure of activities.

THE CONCEPTS

The rationale for this approach has been expressed in a
number of simple, clear explanations of the psychological
causes of drug addiction and how the therapeutic community
will enable life to be lived without drugs.   These explanations are known as 'the concepts'.   They picture drug
addicts as people with a particular kind of personality:
anxious and self-doubting, needing to convince themselves and
others of a success that isn't real and so unable to risk
close, honest relationships, leading impulsive self-centred
lives oblivious of the people around them except when they
can be used to meet the addict's own needs.   The concepts
minimise the importance of family, social and economic factors.   These may have contributed to the addict's plight,
but it is he or she who is responsible for the response to
these conditions.   No one has to be a drug addict, so it is
up to the individual to choose, and to change.

The availability of simple, direct concepts, rather than
the more tentative or complex theories which professionals
tend to use (such as psychoanalysis) helps residents to experience a sense of mastery over their previously helpless
situation.   (An interesting parallel to this was Maxwell
Jones lecturing his effort syndrome patients on the physiology of their symptoms.)   Being able to understand and
explain to others how one's difficulties were caused is of
considerable value in motivating someone for the effort that
personal change involves.   Indeed it is probably one of the
key elements in all self-help movements and in many religious
movements too.

The concepts can be grouped into three sorts: those which
explain the nature of the addict's problems, those which
demonstrate how therapy works, and those which underline how
he ought (and ought not) to conduct himself in the community.
You may wonder how the same explanations can apply equally to
everyone.   The answer seems to be that they are sufficiently
general, and that drug addicts have sufficient experiences in
common, for this to be effective.   The latter point is
important - addicts share many common experiences and psychological characteristics.   The concepts would not necessarily
apply to a wider cross-section of psychologically disturbed
people.

Here are some examples: (3)

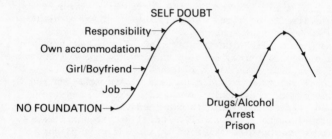

Figure 5.1   The roller coaster

This concept explains to the new resident the pattern of
his life prior to joining the community, and makes sense of
his failure to achieve success and stability up till now.
It shows how temporary enthusiasm leads to short-lived
achievements, but without a foundation (of self-knowledge)
the responsibilities cannot be borne.   Anxiety and self-
doubt lead to things going wrong and before he knows it he is
back on drugs and in trouble with the law.   The cycle
repeats itself, getting worse each time.

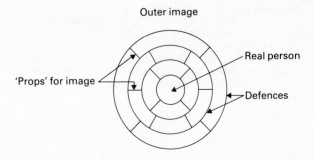

Figure 5.2   The onion

This concept illustrates the kind of defence many addicts
use to distance themselves from other people.   Addicts are
often 'image' conscious young people - e.g. appearing to be
tough, aloof, cool, relaxed, etc.   The onion concept explains that such appearances are a protection against letting
others see them, or even against seeing themselves, as they
really are.   The 'props' for an image might include styles
of dress, hair, 'street talk', and so on.   In the therapeutic community these props are taken away - residents are required, for example, to dress in a fairly conventional way -
so that these image-defences can be broken through and the
real person revealed.

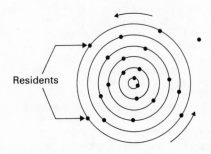

Figure 5.3   The community wheel

This explains something about life in the therapeutic community, which is compared to a spinning wheel.   New residents are on the outside at first and at risk of being spun
off.   They have to work their way into the centre by involving themselves in everything that goes on.   Those near the
centre are more stable and less likely to 'fly off'.   There
is a community wheel on the wall with every resident's name
on it.   Residents can move each other's names according to
where they feel that person is at the time.

Act as if

This is one of the most important concepts, instructing residents on how they should behave in the community.   It is explained that much of the addict's problems come from acting
impulsively, according to the feelings of the moment.   In
the community they are expected to learn self-control.
While working they should not let irritation or frustrations
show, and should act in a calm, tolerant, cordial manner.
The place to deal with the feelings is in the encounter
groups.   Such an injunction makes sense when seen as an
antidote to the addict's prior failure to cope with frustration.   It is, in effect, teaching residents how to function
despite their impulses and feelings.

THE STRUCTURE OF ACTIVITIES

The style of operation evolved at Synanon in the late 1950s
and 1960s set the pattern for all its successors.   Today
staff from concept-based communities around the world can
meet and discuss their work with some certainty that their
communities resemble each other in their overall structure
and the terms they use.   The main features include total
drug abstinence, a hierarchical work structure, encounter
groups modelled on the 'Synanon', and a range of education
and social activities.   In addition to these basic elements,
there is an overall atmosphere or culture of close mutual
surveillance and intense pressure on everyone to be actively
engaged with and concerned for others.   Some communities
have also incorporated a variety of experiential group techniques associated with that other Californian export, the
personal growth movement.

Drug abstinence

Because the communities are primarily for ex-drug addicts who
want to learn to live without drugs, abstinence from all
mind-affecting drugs - including alcohol - is a cardinal
rule.   The possibility of social drinking is not entertained
during the residents' treatment.   Communities differ as to
whether they condone it in the later phases of rehabilitation.   The attitude to the use of illegal drugs, including
cannabis, is clear cut - any use is unacceptable by staff or
residents.   This attitude derives from the view that it is
the drug-taking sub-culture, not the drug itself, which is
the chief enemy, and that drug use inevitably involves contact with this sub-culture.   In order to emphasise this
rule, and make it easier to enforce, no drugs or alcohol are
allowed on the premises.   Prospective residents are interviewed away from the community and new residents are searched
on arrival.   Some communities extend the ban on addictive
substances to cigarettes.

Hierarchical work structure

Residents are responsible for the entire day-to-day servicing
of the community, to an exacting level of precision and tidi-
ness.   Communities are often situated in large houses which
have seen better days and offer considerable scope for maintenance work.   The work is carried out and supervised
through a hierarchy of residents, carefully structured so
that each position has defined duties and each level carries
wider responsibilities than the one below it.   In contrast
to the democratic-analytic communities the structure is
designed to heighten the differences between each level of
responsibility.   The hierarchy applies only during work, not
to relationships outside work time.

The following, based on the Ley Community in Oxford, is
probably fairly typical for a community of 20-30 residents.

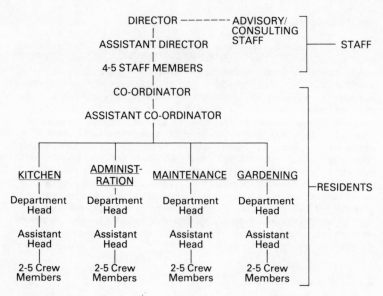

Figure 5.4 Example of hierarchy in a concept-based therapeutic community

This hierarchy has a number of functions. The precise expectations of task performance are in marked contrast to the life style of most drug addicts. The structure provides an antidote for people whose lives have been very disorganised before joining the community. The hierarchy is also an achievable status system. Whereas in society most drug addicts fail to achieve any position of success, in the therapeutic community they can climb from being a crew member engaged in menial jobs to becoming the co-ordinator with responsibility and prestige. A resident can eventually become a staff member and director of a community. The hierarchy also symbolises the autocratic family of which Dederich spoke. Those at the bottom are the 'babies' with no responsibilities for others. Those halfway up are like older brothers and sisters, with responsibility for their younger 'siblings', while those at the top are the adults or parents of the family. Lastly the hierarchy is a very practical preparation for work in the outside world, of which few addicts will have had much experience.

Each department is fully responsible for one aspect of the day-to-day running of the community. On arrival new resi-

dents are put into one of the work crews where they are expected to carry out instructions willingly and respectfully,
and to be aware of what they are doing.   Many addicts take
little notice of their surroundings, and new residents are
often told to go over the job they have just done in order to
make them attend to every detail.   Crew members are also expected to converse while working, not to use work as an
escape from relationships.   The supervisor (assistant head
of department) notices and 'passes up' information on the
crew members' work performance and on their attitudes and
social behaviour.   The head of the department is responsible
for organising the work, deciding what, how and when tasks
should be done, and for passing up information to the co-
ordinator.   Such responsibility can be quite stressful.   A
department head who makes a mess of things may be 'shot down'
- i.e. demoted back to the level of crew member so as to re-
learn the simpler levels of responsibility, and have time to
sort themselves out before having another go at a responsible
position.

The co-ordinator and assistant co-ordinator are responsible for keeping in touch not only with the progress of the
different departments but with the attitudes and behaviour of
all the residents.   If someone is being slack, rude, or
otherwise not conforming they may be called into the co-ordinator's office for a 'talking to' or a 'haircut' - a verbal
dressing down.   The co-ordinator informs the staff of any
problems and asks their advice about dealing with difficulties.   The staff go through the co-ordinator and heads of
departments in organising activities and implementing decisions.   It is important for maintaining the hierarchy that
the staff are seen to go through the 'proper channels' rather
than approach crew members directly.

One consequence of the hierarchy is that a relatively
small number of staff can manage the community, for their job
is less to provide the therapeutic relationships themselves
than to maintain the community's culture at its optimum.   At
best the community functions rather like a well-tuned engine,
but there are a number of ways in which it can start to
falter.   Too much pressure to conform may cause residents to
leave, or find covert ways of opting out.   Too little pressure may lead to a loss of group cohesion and commitment.
Many residents will be quick to spot loopholes in a system
and exploit them.   The effectiveness of this kind of community requires that there be few loopholes or escape routes
(other than leaving).   Constant surveillance by the staff
and swift response to deviant behaviour are needed to keep

the 'engine' running well.   It also provides an important
demonstration of the staff's sincerity and interest.   Even
negative attention may be valued.   One resident told me he
was worried that he had not had a 'haircut' for two months,
as he thought this meant the others were not really interested in him.

Encounter groups

This term has a wide contemporary usage, but in concept-based
communities it refers to the type of verbally aggressive 'no
holds-barred' group developed at Synanon.   These provide an
essential balance to the structured working relationships.
The work hierarchy creates pressures which bring to the surface feelings and attitudes which can be discharged and then
examined in the encounter groups.

    The groups may be held two or three times a week, lasting
for 2-3 hours, sometimes longer.   There may be two or three
simultaneous groups each with ten or twelve residents.   Membership is not constant but is decided on the basis of which
residents need to be in the same group together to deal with
their present relationships.   (This practice is in contrast
to the democratic-analytic communities in which regular group
membership is considered necessary.   This leads members to
develop a strong attachment to 'their' small group, whereas
in a concept-based community the main attachment is to the
community as a whole.)

    The encounter group follows an established procedure.   In
the first phase several members confront a particular individual over some aspect of his or her recent behaviour or
attitude.   The indictments are made at ear-splitting volume.
For example, the crew members of one of the work departments
may shout and curse at their supervisor (violence and threats
are forbidden) whose instructions were confusing or inconsis-
tent.   The supervisor may in turn scream back at them for
being lazy or sloppy, or may decide to sit there and brave it
out.   This phase is intended to break through the individual's defensive barrier, while also allowing tensions to be
discharged.   There follows a phase of frank, probing discussion of the difficulties which the resident is having in the
community at that time.   For example, a male resident in the
position of supervisor may be feeling lonely and isolated,
afraid that if he behaves in an authoritative way, others
won't like him.   Following this phase of the encounter several others may share their own similar feelings, and the

resident is finally given some advice about how to cope with
immediate difficulties.   This often includes a re-affirma-
tion of the commitment to stay in the community and get more
involved with the other members.   The group then passes on
to focus on another member and the shouting begins again.

These groups can appear daunting to the newcomer - a new
resident may take some weeks before learning to bellow out
feelings with full force.   They may seem to be a vehicle for
scapegoating, but emphasis is placed on the need for confrontation to come from concern for the other person rather than
rejection.   In fact the encounter group can generate considerable warmth and closeness between its members.   In a sense
they are an initiation ceremony into intimacy.   Once residents have been through the hail of verbal attacks they may
start to feel much closer to one another than they could
otherwise have done.

Social confidence training

Another range of activities are intended to give residents
the general knowledge, skills and confidence which they have
previously lacked to deal with social situations.   There are
frequent seminars when one resident gives a talk to the
others on a subject which the resident has prepared in
advance.   These will include presentation of the concepts to
new residents.   There are impromptu speaking sessions when
residents take it in turns to stand up and speak on a topic
without any preparation.   The more experienced residents go
out on speaking engagements, when they describe the work of
the community and their own life histories to audiences from
interested organisations.   And there are the daily morning
meetings.   These are not unstructured community meetings but
a cross between school assembly and party games.   Announce-
ments are made, backsliders are spotlighted, belief in the
value of the community is re-affirmed, and then some members
will be expected to drop their 'image' and entertain the
others with a funny song or act.   I can say from experience
that this is good for inhibited professionals as well as ex-
addicts.

Relating

In addition to coping with these rather formal social situations, residents are expected to spend much of their free
time 'relating' to each other in pairs, talking about their

feelings and getting to know the other person.   Spare time -
after meals or in the morning - is not to be spent alone.
Opportunities for relating to outsiders occur on 'open house'
days when relatives and local people are invited in.   Such
events occasion a good deal of nervousness among the residents who, having grown to feel at ease with each other, need
to test out their social skills with other people.

Phases of treatment

Most concept-based communities operate a series of phases of
treatment, although the exact number may vary.   The description given so far applies to the phase or phases when the
resident is living, working and relating to others exclusive-
ly in the community.   This may last around twelve months.
In the next phase he looks for a job outside and begins to go
out in the evening while still living in the community.   In
the last phase, he leaves, often getting a flat or house with
residents who are leaving at the same time.   At a later date
if he has stayed 'clean' and kept within the law he will
become a 'graduate' of the community.   Some communities mark
graduation with a special dinner and a graduation ring,
modelling themselves on the American college.

SOME ISSUES

There is little doubt that concept-based therapeutic communities are controversial in ways that other therapeutic communities are not.   They have what amounts to a complete hand-
book of behaviour, attitudes and values, which applies to
everything that goes on in the community from getting up in
the morning to relaxing in the evening.   They use a wide
array of methods for inducing conformity and commitment, some
of which have earned criticism.   They have been regarded as
a cultural breakthrough by some, as a dangerous cult by
others.   Synanon's antecedents include one of the less
savoury moral crusades of this century.   And relations
between staff who are ex-addicts and those with professional
backgrounds have been less than polite in the United States,
although elsewhere are perhaps rather better.   Let us look
at these issues in turn.

Pressures to conform

Much of my description has implied the use of rewards and
punishments, although these terms are seldom used within a
community. The communities themselves see a 'haircut'
(verbal dressing down) or 'shooting someone down' the hierarchy not as punishment but as giving the individual greater
self-awareness. Promotion to a new position is seen less as
a reward than as an opportunity to 'stretch out' and acquire
greater skills and self-confidence. From this point of view
what matters is that such events have an understandable meaning for the resident, and do not repeat his experience of a
hostile world simply handing out punishment to a resentful
offender.

    This needs to be said because concept-based communities
have sometimes had a 'bad press' for some of their ways of
dealing with serious transgressions of the community's norms
such as stealing or using drugs. These have included shav-
ing a man's head (women wear stocking caps) or hanging a
placard around someone's neck, with words on it which describe his problem in stark terms, e.g. 'I steal things
because I can't ask for love. Please help me.' The purpose of such measures is to shock the individual into awareness of the seriousness of his problem. However, they can
also seem to the outsider as degrading and humiliating, and
relatives of residents and well-meaning professionals have
sometimes been indignant at their use. Some communities
have given them up in favour of less controversial devices.
The important point, however, is how they are seen by the
persons involved. In a community where there is an atmosphere of concern, to which the individual is responsive, they
may be felt as acceptable forms of penance, to change attitudes and behaviour. In the absence of such an atmosphere,
they may only be humiliating and the outsider's viewpoint
might be nearer the mark.

    In addition to these dramatic acts there are a wide range
of more conventional privileges and sanctions which are in
effect a system of rewards and punishments. Permission to
write and receive letters, to go out alone, or spend time on
favourite interests, are all privileges controlled by the
staff. By withdrawing all such rights at first, the new
resident is pushed into total involvement with the community.
(The pioneers of moral treatment in the nineteenth century
had the same idea, and forbade new patients contact with the
outside world, especially with close relatives as they were
considered to be part of the problem.) Once the resident

has established a secure bond with the community (the 'baby'
stage has been passed) he is given his 'privileges' and can
begin to move out into the wider world.

Despite these and other devices for inducing conformity
and commitment, it is likely that none of them is actually as
potent as the relationships between residents.   While residents in their first few months may go through the motions of
showing concern for others, eventually this becomes quite
genuine.   Being physically held and accepted by another
resident while the most painful and frightening feelings are
being experienced creates feelings of great closeness and
trust.   After six months residents may feel closer to their
peers than they have ever felt to anyone in their lives.
Such mutual concern or love is a far more powerful influence
on behaviour than the formal system of sanctions.   The confrontation of a resident for a 'bad attitude' comes then, not
from dutiful conformity, but from a concern that both the
confronter and the confronted should 'make it through the
programme' together.

Cultural breakthrough or cult?

In his book 'Daytop Village' sociologist Barry Sugarman
claims that concept houses have managed to combine two conflicting aspects of American and Western culture.   One is
the 'Protestant Ethic' - 'the notion that man should strive
to overcome any obstacles to his ambitions lying either in
the physical environment or within himself.'   The other is
altruism, showing concern for others, which has 'always been
a major element in the Judaeo-Christian humanist tradition.'
Sugarman points out that these two values, ambition and concern for others, are usually in opposition to one another.
He gives as an example the 'hippie' movement of the 1960s
which was a rejection of the Protestant Ethic in favour of
altruistic values.   In an almost unique way, he says, concept-based therapeutic communities have 'brought together the
emphasis on mastery of one's own life situation and the value
of altruism, an achievement of profoundly important implications, which explains the fascination that Synanon, Daytop,
etc., have exercised over many visitors.'

Cultural breakthrough!   Yet Synanon itself also came to
exemplify another feature of American culture: the existence
of numerous sects and cults of a religious or semi-religious
nature.   The background to Synanon is of interest here.
Dederich and the other founders of Synanon were all members

of Alcoholics Anonymous and many features of AA were carried
over into the new organisation.   Alcoholics Anonymous, like
Synanon, fosters an intense feeling of fellowship between
members through the open discussion of personal histories and
problems.   It offers a clear series of steps to follow to
recovery, and gives the recovered alcoholic the identity of a
valued person who can help others.   A major influence on
Alcoholics Anonymous, and through it on Synanon and the concept-based therapeutic communities, was a movement known as
the Oxford Group.   This was a religious movement devoted to
spiritual rebirth founded at the beginning of the twentieth
century by a young American Lutheran minister, Frank Buchman.
(The connection with Oxford seems tenuous.   Buchman reported
having had a mystical experience in the English town of Kes-
wick, and later having taught near Oxford.)   The Oxford
Group grew to become an international organisation, changing
its name to the First Christian Fellowship and then in 1938
to Moral Re-armament.   Under this name it became linked to
the United States' crusade against communism in the 1950s -
the infamous McCarthy era.   Rather less has been heard of it
of late. (4)

From our point of view the interest of the Oxford Group
lies in some of its principles, which foreshadowed those of
concept-based therapeutic communities.   These included the
open confession of misdeeds in group meetings, atoning for
misdeeds by making restitution to those you have wronged,
dramatic conversion to a new set of convictions which guaran-
tee a trouble-free future, and accepting guidance for all
one's actions from the divinely inspired authority of the
leader.   In many ways this is the stuff of all evangelical
sects.   The Oxford Group's distinguishing feature, which it
imparted to Alcoholics Anonymous and Synanon, was the practice of group confession of personal failure, and total openness and honesty between group members.   Synanon started as
a therapeutic community, but came increasingly to resemble
its predecessor, the Oxford Group.   In so doing it changed
from a therapeutic community to a religious cult community.

This raises the question of what the differences are
between a cult community and a therapeutic one.   There are
sufficient similarities to give some grounds for confusion
between the two.   Both are often started and led by someone
with personal 'charisma'; both claim to help those who feel
psychologically and socially inadequate; both seek to create
in their members a high level of commitment to the community;
and both operate in some degree of isolation from the outside
world.   The differences are in the aims of the community,

what is offered to members and expected in return, and the
way control is exercised.

The aim of many 'cult' communities is to establish an
ideal life style in which negative human qualities such as
greed or jealousy disappear.   Some may also want to convert
others, spread the gospel, or attack outsiders who appear unsympathetic.   Members are promised a complete and lasting
solution to life's problems, in return for complete acceptance of the cult's philosophy and practices.   Leadership
and decisions about the community are usually not openly discussed, and may often be determined by a single person or
small group whose authority is not open to question.

In contrast the aims of a therapeutic community are concerned primarily with individuals, and with establishing a
culture in which individual change is possible.   Complete
solutions are not offered.   Residents are expected to leave
eventually, having learned to cope better with the many problems they still have to face.   Rules and expectations do not
require total and immediate acceptance - indeed this would be
anti-therapeutic - but are regarded as a testing ground for
the resident's subsequent relationships with authority and
society.   Decisions may or may not be taken democratically
by the whole community, according to the kind of therapeutic
community, but can be freely discussed and challenged in
group meetings.

What safeguards are there against a therapeutic community
developing into a cult?   The lessons of Synanon suggest at
least two important ones.   One is to maintain an openness to
people and ideas from outside the community, to listen to and
meet critics rather than regard them as enemies.   The other
is to maintain a forum within the community in which the way
decisions are made and authority is exercised can be regularly examined and questioned.   In effect this is to suggest
that all therapeutic communities need to have an effective
element of democracy at least amongst the staff.

Ex-addicts and professional staff

Ex-addicts who have successfully completed their own rehabilitation can work as staff members in concept-based communities.   Indeed it is the presence of staff who were once
addicts themselves that gives these therapeutic communities
their unique credibility in the field of addiction treatment.

In practice, however, ex-addict staff will often be working alongside professionally qualified staff because it is the latter who are in a position to organise treatment projects, to get funds and to hire staff.   Synanon was created by ex-addicts on their own, but few communities have the organising genius of a Dederich.   There are also, I believe, advantages in having a mixed staff team in which ex-addicts and professional staff balance each other's contribution and points of view.

The ex-addict's personal experience of the damaging, potentially lethal, effects of drug addiction makes them strongly committed to helping others learn to live without drugs.   It also makes them quick to recognise the persuasive deceipts and rationalisations that addicts use with professional helpers.   Having been through such a community themselves they can empathise with what residents are feeling, and (most important from the resident's point of view) the ex-addict staff member offers a living example of someone like themselves who has succeeded in making a life without drugs.

Professional staff can contribute the 'outsider' perspective of alternative views and experience.   At a personal level being 'straight' - not a former member of the drug sub-culture - offers another useful role model to staff and residents alike.   Ex-addict staff may preserve a stereotyped picture of 'straight' people as dull and conventional but also as emotionally untroubled.   Personal contact can break down this stereotype and show that 'straights' have problems too.   Professionals can also contribute to the ideas which the staff use in their work, and can help to create the kind of forum I mentioned above for examining authority issues. A regular meeting of ex-addict and professional staff at the Ley Community in Oxford has enabled the staff there to discuss problems in a more open and non-judgmental way.

There is a risk in such a mixed staff team that the basic principles of the community will be eroded, and it is important that the concepts and hierarchical structure are not undermined.   One of the difficulties in bringing together the beliefs of a successful method of self-help therapy and the scientific tradition of questioning and analysing ideas is that the beliefs will be weakened.   Although the 'concepts' may not provide a completely accurate picture of addiction and its cure, belief in them is essential as a way of helping residents to make sense of their experience.   The same applies to many self-help movements and it is important that professionals working with them appreciate this. (5)

More tangible problems have also occurred in the working
relationships between professional and ex-addict staff.   Ex-
addicts lack the social status and salaries of qualified professionals, and although much has been done in some countries
to create a career structure for ex-addicts they may still
feel with justification that they are treated as second-class
professionals.   Conflicts may occur over who should be in
overall control of a community, as happened at Daytop.
There may also be mutual suspicion, professionals seeing ex-
addicts as untrustworthy, and ex-addicts seeing professionals
as prejudiced and ill-informed.   Some of both groups will
prefer to work without the problems of collaboration, but the
surest development of concept-based communities probably
rests in the attempt to combine the perspectives of both
types of staff.

Chapter 6
Alternative asylum and anti-psychiatry

Individuals in need of psychological help or refuge have not
always turned for help to psychiatry and its allied professions.   Religious communities have provided alternative care
for the psychologically disabled for many centuries.   The
first was probably at Geel in Belgium, which became a special
place of pilgrimage for 'lunatics' in the fourteenth century. (1)   In recent times communities for the mentally handicapped and for maladjusted children have been established
by several Christian organisations.   The best known of these
are probably associated with the work of Rudolf Steiner, the
Austrian teacher-philosopher who created a movement known as
Anthroposophy.   He established a number of educational principles which, although rather different from those of most
therapeutic communities, are today applied in a number of
schools and communities whose aims are similar. (2)   An
example is the international network of Camphill Village Communities for mentally handicapped children and adults.
These communities and others like them provide a home for
many people who would otherwise be in state institutions of
one sort or another.

Although such communities bear an obvious similarity to
other therapeutic communities - valuing the open expression
of feelings, the development of personal relationships, and
the equal sharing of daily tasks - in other respects they
differ from them.   There is relatively little emphasis on
the use of groups for therapeutic purposes and relatively
little exploration of conflicts between members or of the unconscious and defensive aspects of relationships.

Until twenty or so years ago religious communities of one
one kind or another were probably the only alternative to
psychiatric institutions for people who needed a healing

environment away from everyday society. In the past two
decades there has been a huge growth in the number of alternative groups and organisations for people suffering from
many kinds of physical, psychological and social handi-
caps. (3) Concept-based therapeutic communities, described
in the previous chapter, belong to this growth, which reflec-
ted the much wider social changes taking place in the 1960s.
This was the decade in which established authority in many
forms - medicine, education, the police, politicians - came
under attack. It was the decade of flower power and student
protest, of alternative life styles in communes and religious
sects, of alternative therapies such as meditation, LSD, and
encounter groups. Within this social climate there emerged
a number of 'causes célèbres': one was anti-psychiatry.

'Anti-psychiatry' was the name given to a view of psychiatry which became a kind of crusade in the late 1960s and
early 1970s. Although its passion as a movement has waned
over the last decade, it remains a touchstone - a source of
what to believe - for many people working in the field of
mental health, in particular for those who work in therapeutic communities. Its chief concern was with beliefs and
ideas: about the nature of mental illness, about the role of
psychiatrists and the hospitals they work in, and about what
constitutes 'normal' behaviour in society. But anti-psychiatry gave rise also to a number of practical projects intended to help those who were actual or potential psychiatric
patients. Among these projects were small communities and
households which provided an alternative form of asylum to
psychiatric hospitals. In some respects they took therapeutic community principles and extended them beyond the walls,
and the limitations, of the psychiatric hospital.

Today the revolutionary nature of these households has
been lessened by recent developments in community psychiatry,
but they remain at the far end of a spectrum which starts
from the highly structured concept-based communities through
the democratic-analytic type, to those with as little structure as possible. More than the other types of therapeutic
communities described in this book, those which emerged from
the anti-psychiatry movement were the product of ideas rather
than chance combinations of circumstances. They were conscious attempts to put into practice the theories of their
founders. To understand them, therefore, we have to understand the ideas behind them.

THE BASIC IDEAS

In 1967 two British psychiatrists, Ronald Laing and David
Cooper, both published books which launched a vehement attack
on conventional hospital-based psychiatry, in particular on
the treatment of patients labelled as schizophrenic.
Cooper's book, 'Psychiatry and Anti-Psychiatry', gave the new
movements its name, and Laing's 'Politics of Experience'
became required reading for a generation of young people for
whom 'inner experience' was elevated to a way of life, com-
memorated in Timothy Leary's famous slogan 'turn on, tune in,
drop out'.   A year either side of 1967, a French psychoanalyst Jaques Lacan and an Italian psychiatrist Franco
Basaglia, also published books which became landmarks in an
international anti-psychiatry movement. (4)   In the United
States the psychoanalyst Thomas Szasz published a string of
books in the 1960s and 1970s with such resounding titles as
'The Myth of Mental Illness' and 'The Manufacture of Madness'.   What were all these doctors saying?

   Despite their differences they were all concerned with a
common dilemma: 'whose side is the psychiatrist on'?   Is
his job to help the patient become a whole, healthy autono-
mous individual, or is it to preserve the social peace by
getting patients to fit in with the way others want them to
be?   Does he serve the patient or society?

   The problem was not new.   Freud was well aware of it, and
any psychiatrist who has had to decide whether to admit a
patient to hospital against his will has had to face it.   A
conventional way out of the dilemma has been to include the
patient's resistance to treatment as one of the symptoms of
his illness - a strategy roundly condemned by the anti-psychiatrists.   If the patient's unwillingness to be treated is
not seen as part of the illness the rights and wrongs of the
situation become harder to judge, and the psychiatrist may
feel he is being put in the role of jailer or policeman if he
forces the patient to have treatment.

   In response to such ethical problems the anti-psychiatrists had little doubt.   Their responsibility was to the
patient only.   They were not there to be jailers or police-
men, to persuade the patient to behave in a socially acceptable way, or to make life easier for the patient's relatives
or society in general.   They were there to help people who
were temporarily overwhelmed by life's difficulties, to guide
them through the turmoil of their breakdown till they found
their way again.   Some anti-psychiatrists rejected completely

the idea of mental illness.   They saw it as a concept with little intrinsic value, only useful as a justification for giving patients treatments they didn't want to have.   Most accepted that peculiar states of mind, which we call madness or psychosis, do exist, but that these states provide no reason for ostracising people or taking control over their lives.   Some emphasised the need to make special provision for people experiencing such states of mind, so that they could go through them without interference.   Others stressed the need for active efforts to deal with the problems that produced the breakdown by working in the setting where it first arose - the family and the neighbourhood.

These views led anti-psychiatrists to withdraw from prac-tising psychiatry in conventional settings, because they would inevitably be on the side of society, or at least caught between conflicting interests.   Psychiatric hospitals in particular were seen as beyond any hope of real improve-ment, too tainted by their function of holding people against their will, or simply by their institutional codes of conduct which inhibited the spontaneity and autonomy of staff and patients alike.   To the anti-psychiatrists even therapeutic communities could not offer real freedom from these con-straints as long as they were based in hospitals.   The staff in hospital-based therapeutic communities are often prepared to tolerate these limitations, or try to change them from within.   The anti-psychiatrists were not.   They were criti-cal not only of hospitals but of psychotherapists who pur-sued goals of social adjustment and conformity with their patients, rather than using therapy purely as a means to greater self-knowledge and autonomy.

In addition to this central concern about the role of the psychiatrist and the goals of psychiatric treatment, two re-lated issues were of vital importance to anti-psychiatry: the true nature of what we call schizophrenia, and the rela-tionship between mental illness and the way society itself functions.

An important idea in the setting up of alternative asylums was that psychosis - schizophrenia in particular - was not an illness to be cured but a remarkable inner journey to be guided through.   The schizophrenic was someone who, without wishing to, had embarked on a voyage back to his earliest experiences and his inner self.   Once embarked, what he needed was the presence of others who could look after him and guide him through the experience until he returned, 'reborn' as it were.   Evidence for this heroic view of schiz-

ophrenia was found in the way similar experiences were treated in other cultures and other periods of history: healing
rituals had often involved a kind of spiritual journey and
rebirth.   Laing wrote

> under all circumstances a man may get stuck, lose himself,
> and have to turn round and go back a long way to find him-
> self again.   Only under certain socio-economic conditions
> (i.e. present-day Western society) will he be said to
> suffer from schizophrenia. (5)

The implication of this view was that psychiatric treatments
like drugs and ECT actually prevented recovery, since they
stopped the 'journey'.   What was needed was some special
provision, a place where people could go to have a breakdown. (6)   This view led to the setting up of Kingsley Hall,
the first anti-psychiatry community, which is described
below.

Here is not the place to evaluate the treatment of schizophrenia.   Its nature, causes and cures will be the subject
of debate within psychiatry for many years to come.   Yet
there is evidence that for some people who experience a psychotic breakdown, in which for a while they become helpless
and dependent on others, the anti-psychiatry approach can
enable them to recover without physical treatment. (7)

The anti-psychiatrists' view of the relationship between
mental illness and society also takes us into realms which
are beyond the scope of this book to explore in depth.
Briefly, there are two arguments.   One, particularly associated with the work of Laing, states that living in modern
Western society is so damaging to our true spontaneous
natures that becoming 'mentally ill' may actually be a heal-
thier response than staying 'normal'.   The other argument,
more political and associated with the writings of Marxist
psychiatrists such as Cooper and the French anti-psychiatrists, is that those who are called mentally ill are the
victims of a conspiracy by society to deny the truth of what
they are saying.   The patient's illness is seen as a social
or political protest, and psychiatric treatment is equated
with political repression.   Both arguments have a point, and
there is no doubt that the second is literally true in some
countries, such as the Soviet Union.   How far you go along
with these arguments depends largely on your own political
view of the world.

In its style and rhetoric anti-psychiatry appeals to those

looking for an anti-establishment ideology to believe in. Shorn of its poetry and politics it loses some of its attractiveness but contains ideas which have had a pronounced effect on conventional psychiatry.   In England and the United States, for example, techniques such as crisis intervention and family therapy, which have grown rapidly over the past ten years, have been influenced by the anti-psychiatrists' views on avoiding hospital admission and treating the whole family.   In Italy, Basaglia's work has led to the bold move to close down psychiatric hospitals entirely and replace them with networks of neighbourhood mental health centres.

Yet to point to the ways in which anti-psychiatry has influenced the practice of conventional psychiatry risks missing what it was really about, for it was and remains much more about beliefs and values than about practical ways of doing things.   It was an attempt to extend our view of psychological 'breakdown' to include its spiritual, social and political dimensions.   It pointed out that the concept of 'illness' was far too restricting to enable us fully to understand madness, and reminded us that psychiatrists now deal with the problems that were once the domain of priests. While modern psychiatric techniques can offer speedy relief to those in distress, there may be some for whom other healing rituals are still more appropriate.   No doubt the anti-psychiatrists overstated their case when they claimed that only they understood the 'truth' about madness and that their approach was best for everyone.   Yet their exaggerated claims were perhaps an indication of the extent to which it seemed that these other dimensions of mental illness had been hitherto neglected.

The therapeutic community pioneers in the 1940s and 1950s had set themselves the target of trying to change psychiatry from within - with some success.   The anti-psychiatrists of the 1960s and 1970s went a stage further and proposed that some radical new alternative to the psychiatric establishment was needed.   The first and still perhaps the best-known attempt to put this proposal into practice was Kingsley Hall.

ANTI-PSYCHIATRY IN PRACTICE

Before Kingsley Hall: a failed experiment

David Cooper, in the early 1960s, had already experimented in taking a therapeutic community in a psychiatric hospital beyond the usual limits of tolerance for non-conformity.

Patients had been free to get up when they chose and attend
as much or as little of the daily programme as they chose.
Staff had restricted the exercise of their authority to the
minimum possible, on the assumption that patients would eventually take responsibility for themselves.   The experiment
did not last very long.   The hospital authorities became
increasingly critical of the state of the ward, and the
staff's anxieties mounted along with the piles of unwashed
plates.   In Cooper's absence the staff decided to reimpose
certain expectations about attendance at meetings and the
length of leave patients could take.   (It is interesting
that untidiness and leave-taking were two of the issues that
also confronted Bion in his original attempt to get patients
to take collective responsibility.   In his case he was successful with the patients but not with the hospital authorities.)   Cooper accepted the staff's decision to reassert
their authority.   He saw this as confirmation that in a hospital it was inevitable that staff would feel too concerned
about the opinions of their colleagues and supervisors to let
such an experiment succeed - as he believed it would if it
went on long enough.   He believed that a true experiment in
allowing patients complete freedom and autonomy in running
their lives could only take place outside the hospital. (8)

Kingsley Hall: a five-year experiment

Kingsley Hall was a large community centre built around the
turn of the century in the heart of London's working-class
East End.   It had been used for many pioneering projects to
help poor people, and the trustees were sympathetic to Laing
and his colleagues, who were looking for somewhere to put
into practice their ideas about an alternative to psychiatric
hospital.

     In 1965 Kingsley Hall was lent to the Philadelphia Assoc-
iation, which had just been formed by Laing and his colleagues.   Between then and 1970, when the lease ran out, 119
people stayed at the Hall.   Most stayed for up to six
months, but a few stayed for a year or more.   One of those
who stayed longer was Mary Barnes, whose written account of
her profound regression to passive helplessness and eventual
recovery has made her one of the celebrities of anti-psychiatry and a key figure in the argument for the Kingsley Hall
approach.   Mary Barnes was one of those - about a third of
the residents - who had previously been treated as a psychiatric in-patient.   Others had been out-patients, and about a
third had no psychiatric history.   Many of these were quali-

fied or trainee psychiatrists and psychotherapists, who
wanted to take part in this experiment in 'unlabelled' l
living.   Of the fifteen to twenty-five people living there
at any one time, only three or four were actually psychotic. (9)

What was Kingsley Hall like?   The visitor was struck by
the run-down appearance of the place, both outside and
inside.   Graffiti in the living room denounced conventional
psychiatric treatments - such as the drug Largactil.   Individuals had their own rooms where they were free to spend as
much time as they wanted.   Some rooms were in quite a
squalid condition.   Joseph Berke, a psychiatrist who lived
in Kingsley Hall, described the way it worked:

> People who were psychotic were given space, they were
> given company if they wished, or not, and they were given
> a great deal of physical support if necessary.   It was a
> feature about life at Kingsley Hall that as people were
> not considered ill, they did not have to be treated.   No
> drugs were given to anybody.   There were no staff and no
> patients, and there was no formal structure of doing
> things around the Hall, yet things got done.   There were
> people who were 'up' and people who were 'down'.   The
> people who were 'up' or capable of functioning in a more
> usual social sense look after the Hall. (10)

The question of how people joined, how things got done,
and the absence of 'staff' and 'patient' roles, were also
discussed by Morton Schatzman:

> If someone wishes to live at Kingsley Hall he must meet
> some or all of the residents first.   Sometimes they
> invite him to stay for an evening meal or a weekend.   The
> residents ask those people to join the community whom they
> like or whom they feel would benefit at Kingsley Hall or
> both.   The residents consider it best for a balance to
> exist between those who are free to deal with ordinary
> social and economic needs - to shop for food, wash dishes,
> scrub floors, clean toilets, stoke the furnace, repair
> broken fuses, and pay the bills - and those who cannot or
> choose not to be, and wish to work upon themselves.... No
> one who lives at Kingsley Hall sees those who perform work
> upon the external material world as 'staff', and those who
> do not as 'patients'.   No caste system forbids people to
> move freely from one sub-group to another, as it does in
> mental hospitals. (11)

Mary Barnes's story illustrates both the possibilities of
success and some of the difficulties and risks involved in
the anti-psychiatrists' approach.   Before coming to Kingsley
Hall in her forties she had been diagnosed as schizophrenic
and had had several periods of hospitalisation, although she
had also been able to work successfully as a nurse in between
them, and had achieved the position of nurse tutor.   She
shared Laing's views on schizophrenia, and was herself seeking the opportunity to experience a complete breakdown without having it treated.   The fact that she was able to 'hold
on' for a year or so until Kingsley Hall was opened suggests
that she had considerable personal resources.   Initially she
continued in her job while living at Kingsley Hall, but then
resigned and allowed herself to regress, without any external
or internal inhibitions.   Later she wrote:

I tore off my clothes, feeling I had to be naked, lay on
the floor with my shits and water, smeared the walls with
faeces.   Was wild and noisy about the house or sitting in
a heap on the kitchen floor.

Schatzman, there at the same time, wrote that: 'others found
it difficult to live with her when she smeared faeces on her
body and on the walls of her room.   Her room was next to the
kitchen and the odour came through the wall.'

Mary Barnes took to lying in her bed all day and refusing
food.   It was at this stage that the anti-psychiatry belief
in non-interference, in giving people total freedom to live
as they chose, came under a severe test.   Joseph Berke
writes that he was horrified when he arrived at Kingsley Hall
after an absence to discover that she was so 'thin that it
was felt that she couldn't even be sent to hospital, as we
might be prosecuted for keeping a person like that'.   An
intense debate took place between Laing and his colleagues,
at which it was recognised that either the principle of complete self-responsibility would have to be sacrificed, or
Mary Barnes might die.   Laing accepted the point and told
her that he wanted her to eat. (12)   Berke began to feed
her, like a baby, with milk from a bottle.   Others took
turns at looking after her, and gradually she began the long
and tortuous journey back to mental and physical health.   As
part of this recovery she expressed her feelings in dozens of
huge vivid paintings.   She and Joseph Berke wrote a joint
book about her experiences at Kingsley Hall, which also
became the subject of a play. (13)

Although Mary Barnes was to become the best known of

Kingsley Hall's residents, she was almost certainly not typical. Few went through such an extreme and protracted period
of 'working on themselves'. Probably more typical were
several whom Schatzman interviewed and described in his
article, Madness and Morals. They were people who in various ways were in a state of personal conflict and stalemate.
They resented having to conform to other people's expectations, but found it impossible in ordinary life to be assertive, aggressive, selfish or rude, in a word, to rebel.
Since there were so few expectations at Kingsley Hall about
what was normal social behaviour and no rules to conform to,
these people could start to do things they would never have
dared to do outside. Here they could decide what they
wanted to do, when they wanted to do it, and be only as
pleasant and sociable as they felt. The anti-psychiatry
principle of not telling people what to do gave them the
freedom they needed to find their own identity. It is
likely that Kingsley Hall, although set up to help those
going through a psychotic breakdown, was more often of help
to young people such as these.

AFTER KINGSLEY HALL

In its five years as a living experiment in anti-psychiatry,
many psychiatrists and other professionals had come to Kingsley Hall to experience the approach at first hand. When it
closed in 1970 some decided to continue its work elsewhere.

In England two new projects were started as alternatives
to psychiatric hospitals. Leon Redler formed the Archway
Community, in a collection of run-down houses in North
London. This later became part of the Philadelphia Association, housing about fifty people in a network of households
in and around London. A second group including Joseph Berke
and Morton Schatzman started the Arbours Association which
now has three long-term communities in London and a short-
term crisis centre. Both associations also offer training
in psychotherapy, utilising residential placements in their
communities as part of the training.

The communities are usually small, housing perhaps 6-10
people, with an atmosphere of laissez-faire permissiveness.
Residents can involve themselves in as much or as little of
the communal life of the house as they wish. The emphasis
is on coming to terms with oneself, usually aided by individual psychotherapy outside the community, more than on social
learning through group involvement. The community is seen
as a 'place to be' rather than as an instrument of therapy.

Two projects are of particular interest.   One is the
Arbours Crisis Centre, which has developed a synthesis of
crisis intervention, psychotherapy and temporary sanctuary. (14)   A team of therapists, some of whom live in the
centre, deal with letters and phone calls from people in emotional crises and offer what help they think is needed.
This can be talking on the telephone, meeting people in their
home, regular individual or family therapy, or offering an
individual or a family a place to stay for a few weeks.   The
therapists believe that with these facilities most levels of
disturbance, including acute psychosis, can be contained and
worked with, without the use of medication.   In the centre
itself, a comfortable, attractively decorated house in North
London, there is little pressure on individuals to conform.
The therapists look after the house and are available round
the clock for informal conversations.   Formal meetings are
held several times a week with those closely involved in the
crisis.   It is a condition of offering someone accommodation
that all those people involved in the crisis are willing to
be involved in these meetings.   The therapists are concerned
to avoid the situation, which often happens with admission to
a psychiatric hospital, where a crisis is resolved by one
person being defined as ill.   They believe that by providing
whatever amount of support and understanding is needed, the
crisis can be contained, the people involved can be calmed, and
the reasons for the crisis can be gone into and resolved.   By
providing the range of facilities it does, the crisis centre
goes beyond anti-psychiatry and in some ways provides a model
for an acute psychiatric service outside hospital.   Indeed,
it seems that the main difference is that the people being
helped should want to seek this kind of alternative to
hospital admission, and be willing to pay something for it.

In the United States a number of projects also took shape
building on the work at Kingsley Hall.   One of these,
Soteria, has combined the anti-psychiatrists' belief in the
self-healing possibilities of certain psychotic states, with
an acceptance of the value of careful research into the success of such a venture when compared with conventional treatment.   Soteria is a large comfortable house in San Francisco,
housing six young schizophrenic patients with six staff working shifts.   The complete equality of roles and absence of
labels of Kingsley Hall has been abandoned, but staff do not
see themselves as therapists and the terminology is contemporary rather than medical: 'spaced out' rather than ill;
'getting it together' rather than getting better.   There is
little formal therapy or structure, but much informal support
and interaction, especially with disturbed newcomers.   There

is acceptance of wide variations in patients' ability to help
with running the house.   In some ways Soteria resembles
hospital-based therapeutic communities of the type described
earlier in this book - especially those caring for acute ad-
missions.   The major differences are: (a) its small size
and homely setting which makes possible more intimacy and cohesiveness than in most hospitals;   (b) the relative absence
of staff control or imposed structure;   and (c) the attempt
to rely on the self-healing nature of psychosis.   The attitude concerning medication is not dogmatic, however, and
drugs are given to those patients - relatively few as it
turns out - who show no change after six weeks.   Comparing
Soteria with conventional in-patient treatments it was found
that Soteria patients not only did better but were more
likely to make the positive step of leaving the parental
home. (15)

It can be argued that anti-psychiatry has, in practice,
become alternative psychiatry.   Alternative forms of support, help and sanctuary have been created for those who want
to avoid either the social consequences of hospital admission, or the use of drugs and ECT as a first rather than last
resort.   No doubt a majority of people will continue to
place their reliance in doctors when under stress, since doctors 'know what to do' in times of crisis.   And most doctors
will continue to place their reliance in forms of treatment
they know and understand - drugs, practical advice, reassur-
ance, and so on.   Alternative psychiatry, like the therapeutic community, deals in another dimension: the interpersonal,
the effects people have on one another.   The assumption that
this is the main dimension in which psychological ailments
occur, and where the work of putting them right must take
place, is not one that has been generally accepted in our
society.

Chapter 7
Summary

Four different kinds of therapeutic community have been described: the institutional, the democratic-analytic, the concept-based and the anti-psychiatry alternative asylum.   In the first chapter I described the elements that I believe they all, to a greater or lesser extent, have in common. The following chapters dealt in some detail with their different origins, beliefs and practices, whom they aim to help and the settings in which they operate.   In summarising I want to underline two things: the distinctive characteristics of each of these four 'types', and the range of possible variations between individual therapeutic communities.   I will try to do this by giving two summary charts.   In the first I have placed the four types side by side and compared them on a number of points (see Table 7.1).

While it has been convenient in writing this book to cluster therapeutic communities into these four groups or types, in practice communities may combine features of two or even three of these types.   For example a psychiatric unit may be influenced by the concept of moral treatment (central to the institutional therapeutic communities) as well as by the theories of democracy and psychoanalysis.   A hostel for ex-psychiatric patients may be influenced by both of these and also by the hierarchical structure which is characteristic of concept-based communities.   A rural community for the handicapped may combine features of an institutional therapeutic community with the 'unlabelled living' of anti-psychiatry's alternative asylum.

It seems appropriate, therefore, to conclude this section of the book by bringing together some of the key ideas which have been referred to in each chapter.   Today all these ideas are available - 'in the air' so to speak - and the

style or culture of any particular therapeutic community will
be influenced by the relative emphasis given to each of them.
Figure 7.1 presents these formative influences in clockwise
order corresponding approximately to the order in which they
have emerged in the 200-year history of therapeutic communities.

TABLE 7.1 Comparisons between four types of therapeutic community

	Institutional	Democratic-analytic	Concept-based	Alternative asylum
Also known as	– therapeutic community approach – social therapy – milieu therapy	– therapeutic community proper – Maxwell Jones type	– concept houses – ex-addict self-help communities – Synanon/Daytop/Phoenix House type	– anti-psychiatry communities – alternative sanctuary – households
Usual settings	– large psychiatric hospitals and associated hostels, group homes, day centres	(a) small specialised psychiatric hospitals (b) special units within large psychiatric hospitals (c) hostels and half-way houses, day hospitals and day centres (d) special schools (e) prison units	– large houses in residential neighbourhoods or rural settings	– houses in residential neighbourhoods or rural settings
Types of residents/ patients	chronic psychiatric patients, usually diagnosed schizophrenic, with moderate to severe social handicaps	(a) younger psychiatric patients with neuroses and personality disorders (b) acute and borderline psychotic patients (c) ex-psychiatric patients (d) maladjusted children and adolescents (e) young offenders	drug abusers (opiates or multiple drug abuse); others with similar problems	people seeking help or refuge following a crisis or breakdown, but wishing to avoid medical treatment and hospitalisation; may sometimes be psychotic

	Institutional	Democratic-analytic	Concept-based	Alternative asylum
Types of staff	the usual mental health professions (psychiatry, nursing, clinical psychology, occupational therapy, social work); also work supervisors, craft instructors, social/remedial therapists	the usual mental health professions; also teachers, psychotherapists, creative therapists (art, music, drama, etc.), hostel wardens, social therapists	ex-addicts who have graduated from similar communities; also usual mental health professions	usually no designated staff; psychotherapists may live in or attend regularly
Usual number of residents/patients	10-20 patients in a psychiatric ward	15-40 residents	15-40 residents; some may be over 100	6-12 residents
Usual length of stay expected	variable - may be few months to years depending on therapeutic goals	around a year, though longer in special schools and shorter in acute psychiatric units	9-18 months	no fixed expectations - may vary from a few weeks to 2-3 years
Procedures				
Participation in running the community	patients participate in decisions about domestic and social ward activities, and take some responsibility for carrying these out	residents/patients/clients participate in decisions about admission, discharge and sanctions, and organise social activities; in non-institutional settings residents take responsibility for catering and domestic work	residents responsible for most aspects of daily administration, catering, maintenance, and for monitoring and reporting fellow residents' behaviour and attitudes	little formal allocation of responsibilities - practical tasks undertaken by those who choose - in practice the therapists and less disturbed residents

Community meetings	- at least once a week, sometimes more frequent - staff tend to take more active role than patients - formal agenda may be used	- daily - staff tend to take less active role than residents - no formal agenda - ad hoc crisis meetings may be called	- daily - run by residents - formal agenda - accoucements, pull-ups, 'image breakers' - staff may call 'general meeting' from time to time if community gets slack	- informal meetings - e.g. at meal times - used to discuss community matters - members of different communities may have occasional 'network' meetings
Other group meetings	- discussion of work activities, assessment of work output - informal group discussion of interests, general knowledge, etc. - specific training and exercises - e.g. social skills, movement and drama, practice for independent living	- verbal group psycho-therapy 2-5 times per week - creative/action therapies - e.g. art, psychodrama - resident business meetings - work groups - selection groups with prospective members - groups for new members, or those planning to leave - family therapy and relatives' meetings	- encounter groups 2-3 times per week - educational seminars - special events including marathon encounter groups lasting 24-48 hours - groups for new residents and those in re-entry phase	- members may meet together once or twice a week with an outside therapist - otherwise no formal group activities, though residents may organise own activities and meetings from time to time

	Institutional	Democratic-analytic	Concept-based	Alternative asylum
Additional therapies	- use of drugs to control psychotic symptoms	some communities (for children or more disturbed adults) combine individual psychotherapy with group activities. Drugs and ECT may be used in acute psychiatric units	no formal individual therapy, but residents are free to ask for individual talks with staff members	in long-term communities members usually have individual psychotherapy outside the community. In shorter-term communities resident therapist(s) may provide round-the-clock individual support

Aims and beliefs

	Institutional	Democratic-analytic	Concept-based	Alternative asylum
Key belief about the common problem shared by patients/residents	Combination of chronic psychosis and institutional living have led to atrophy of social, work and self-care skills, heightened dependency, socially undesirable habits	Neurotic symptoms and deviant behaviour are manifestations of underlying disturbances in interpersonal relationships and distorted perceptions of self, others and society	Drug addiction is a symptom of underlying difficulties in interpersonal relationships and of failure to take responsibility for one's own life	Psychosis indicates that a person has reached an impasse in their life and needs to regress to an earlier self in order to re-emerge as a more complete person
Main therapeutic goals	- reduce socially undesirable behaviour - increase level of functioning in social life, work, self-care - decrease dependency	- reduce symptoms - more realistic perceptions of oneself and others leading to more satisfactory relationships with peers and authority figures	- abstinence from/ reduced use of drugs - absence of criminal activity - ability to establish and maintain close, stable relationships	- re-emergence or 're-birth' from period of regression in more integrated state - being freed from the need to conform to others' expectations, or to impose one's own on others

Main therapeutic ingredients			
– foster tolerant and co-operative peer relations – hospital discharge where possible – increased level of morale within institution as a whole; change from custodial role to rehabilitation – raised levels of expectation about patients' capacities – increased level of general activity – providing patients and staff with opportunities for rewards and personal satisfaction – fostering communication and mutual awareness between patients	– greater confidence in work and social roles – greater social responsibility – involvement in community activities and joint decision-making – receiving feedback and confrontation, about behaviour – taking specific roles and responsibilities – learning through resolution of crises – open discussion and sharing of personal experience, feelings, attitudes – helping others by giving feedback, support, confrontation	– regular work or further study – taking specific roles and responsibilities – acting 'as if' until new attitudes and feelings become internalised – highlighting of authority problems by resident hierarchy – learning explicit set of values and rules of conduct – intense peer group relationships with mutual confrontation and support – open discussion and sharing of personal feelings, experience, attitudes	– becoming autonomous, taking full responsibility for one's own life – freedom to behave as one chooses, absence of rules, expectations, norms – opportunity to regress (for a time) to a state of infantile dependency – allowing the process of regression and recovery to occur without interference by physical treatment – availability of psycho-therapeutic help either intensively over short period or regularly over some months or years

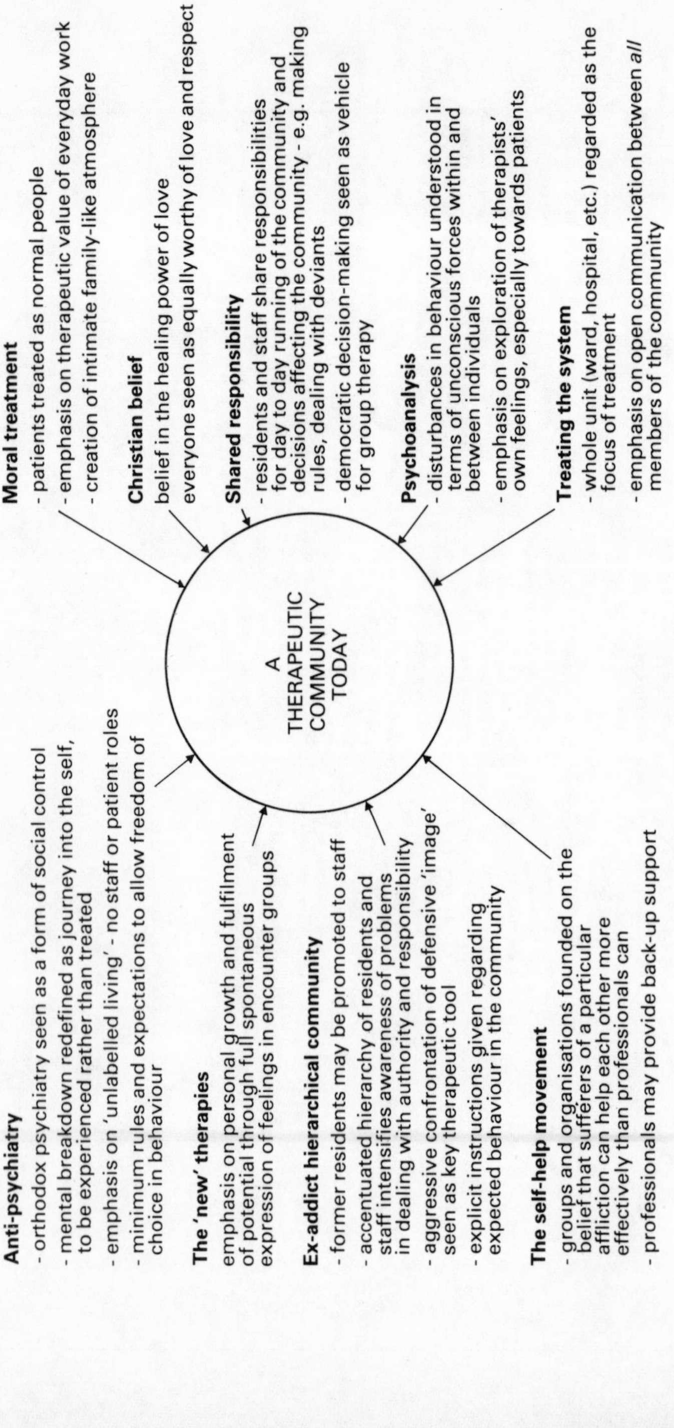

Moral treatment
- patients treated as normal people
- emphasis on therapeutic value of everyday work
- creation of intimate family-like atmosphere

Christian belief
belief in the healing power of love
everyone seen as equally worthy of love and respect

Shared responsibility
- residents and staff share responsibilities for day to day running of the community and decisions affecting the community - e.g. making rules, dealing with deviants
- democratic decision-making seen as vehicle for group therapy

Psychoanalysis
- disturbances in behaviour understood in terms of unconscious forces within and between individuals
- emphasis on exploration of therapists' own feelings, especially towards patients

Treating the system
- whole unit (ward, hospital, etc.) regarded as the focus of treatment
- emphasis on open communication between *all* members of the community

Anti-psychiatry
- orthodox psychiatry seen as a form of social control
- mental breakdown redefined as journey into the self, to be experienced rather than treated
- emphasis on 'unlabelled living' - no staff or patient roles
- minimum rules and expectations to allow freedom of choice in behaviour

The 'new' therapies
emphasis on personal growth and fulfilment of potential through full spontaneous expression of feelings in encounter groups

Ex-addict hierarchical community
- former residents may be promoted to staff
- accentuated hierarchy of residents and staff intensifies awareness of problems in dealing with authority and responsibility
- aggressive confrontation of defensive 'image' seen as key therapeutic tool
- explicit instructions given regarding expected behaviour in the community

The self-help movement
- groups and organisations founded on the belief that sufferers of a particular affliction can help each other more effectively than professionals can
- professionals may provide back-up support

A THERAPEUTIC COMMUNITY TODAY

Figure 7.1 Formative influences on therapeutic communities

Part II

Working in a therapeutic community

Up to this point in the book we have looked at therapeutic communities from the 'outside', at how they started, what they do and what ideas they use. It is also possible to look at them from the inside. What is it like to be in a therapeutic community, as a resident, a staff member or a student? A number of first-hand accounts have been written of the experience of being a resident in a therapeutic community, for example, Mary Barnes at Kingsley Hall and Nick Mahony at the Henderson Hospital. The interested reader is recommended to read these and other accounts for an insight into the resident's experience. (1) The experience of working in a therapeutic community, or being on a student 'placement', has perhaps been less well described. In this part of the book we look at it from two points of view: the immediate impact of arriving in a therapeutic community, and the appropriate training for longer-term staff.

Chapter 8
The first day:
an imaginary narrative

In this chapter I have written an imaginary narrative of three
people spending their first day in a therapeutic community.
It is imaginary in the sense that the people and the community
are fictitious.   The background material for the narrative
was provided by a number of interviews I had with new staff
and trainees in different therapeutic communities, discussing
their reactions to their new situation.   The community itself
is an amalgam of different communities but of necessity had to
have a concrete form.   I have chosen a hospital-based one
because it is the type with which I am most familiar and which
many readers may encounter.   The newcomers, too, represent a
pooling of a wide range of expectations and responses into
three, I hope, believable characters.

*Alexander House is a small psychiatric unit attached to a
larger institution.   The patients, who are referred to as
residents, suffer from a range of psychiatric disorders,
though none are psychotic.   The staff include the normal
psychiatric professions - doctors, nurses, social workers,
etc. - but it will not be immediately apparent who is who in
this respect.   Today three newcomers are arriving.   Their
reasons for coming and their expectations of what it will be
like are different:*

Sue is training to be a general nurse and likes working
with people who are physically ill.   However, her training
requires her to have experience in working in a psychiatric
setting.   She has been told that the place she is going to
is a therapeutic community, but that means little to her.
She's heard from a friend that the staff spend as much time
talking about themselves as they do talking about patients,
which seems peculiar.   But she has an open mind about what
to expect and is willing to make the best of it.

Ian is training to be a social worker.   He enjoys the
group discussions they have on his course and made a point of
asking to spend one of his placements in a therapeutic community.   Unlike Sue he already knows about them from books and
articles, and thinks they are a good thing because they give
everyone an equal vote in decision-making.   Ian doesn't like
hierarchies with professionals at the top and clients at the
bottom, and he sees therapeutic communities as making a political statement about the rights and freedom of those receiving help.

Barbara, unlike Sue and Ian, is not training for a particular occupation.   She took a degree in psychology and was
then unsure what she wanted to do next.   She had a period of
feeling depressed and once saw a psychiatrist who referred
her to a counsellor.   She found this helpful and it led her
to become interested in people with emotional problems.   She
answered an advertisement for a social therapist at Alexander
House and was invited to come for a day.   She has heard a
bit about therapeutic communities and is attracted by the
idea of staff and residents helping one another, without
being the expert.

Let us join Sue, Ian and Barbara as they arrive, as yet un-
acquainted with one another, at Alexander House.   It is 8.20
on a midweek morning.   From the distance it appears set
apart from the neighbouring buildings.   The 'house' is about
the size of a large villa or small hotel.   Approaching the
building two things catch the eye.   There is a broken window
on the ground floor, and two young men, one bearded, are sitting on the grass by the entrance.   Sue is the first to
arrive, and she goes up to them.

'Excuse me, is this Alexander House?'

'Yes, can I help?' answered the man with a beard, not getting up.

'Could you tell me where I could find a member of the
staff?'

'Well, I'm a member of staff.'

'I'm sorry,' Sue was taken aback at the man's casual
manner although he seemed friendly enough, 'I was told to be
here at 8.30.   Can you tell me where I should go?'

'That will be for the staff pre-meeting in the green room. The community meeting starts at 9.'

Sue was digesting this information when the other two newcomers arrived.

'Excuse me,' said Ian to Sue, 'I'm starting here today. Could you tell me where the community meeting is?'

This bewildered Sue even more. Was she the only one who hadn't known there was a community meeting?'

'This is my first day too. . The community meeting starts at 9, but there's something called a pre-meeting at 8.30.'

'That's right,' said the bearded man, standing up, 'I'm going there now. I'll show you the way if you like.'

'Can I come with you?' asked Barbara.

'My name's Nick,' said the bearded man, and they all introduced themselves. As they went in Nick turned to the young man still sitting on the grass.

'Tony, if you want to stay you'll have to explain to the community about why you did that. You know the rules, and I don't see why we should make an exception for you.'

'Crap!' said Tony, not moving from his hunched position.

They went inside and found themselves in a hall with several doors leading off. One or two sleepy-looking people passed them carrying bowls of breakfast cereal. At first sight the inside of the building seemed rather shabby. There were stains on the doors, the carpet was littered with crumbs, and posters showing Greek islands and rock singers were starting to peel from the walls. It certainly doesn't seem like a hospital, thought Sue. There was no one in sight who looked like a member of staff.

Ian was excited. The casual way they were being introduced felt as though they were entering a secret society. He wondered if they were being observed, their reactions being noted. This casual approach is a kind of test, he thought. Barbara trailed behind the others. She would have liked to stay outside and ask Tony what he was angry about. She thought the place looked rather friendly - not like the out-patient clinic she had once attended, with its cold shiny walls and rows of plastic chairs.

They were led through one of the doors and found themselves suddenly in a crowded room.   People were sitting on
chairs, tables and desks, or helping themselves to coffee
from a tray on the floor in the middle of the room.   Several
conversations seemed to be in progress and no one took any
notice of the self-conscious trio standing in the doorway.

'Help yourself to some coffee,' said Nick, and he left
them to go over to a vacant chair on the other side of the
room, leaving them feeling horribly conspicuous yet oddly un-
noticed.   After a moment's hesitation they did as Nick suggested and found places to sit.

'I think we ought to start,' said a middle-aged woman cut-
ting across the hubbub of voices.   'I see we have three newcomers with us today.   Would you like to introduce yourselves?'   The conversation died away and eyes were turned
towards them.   They felt very nervous.

'My name's Ian.   I'm a social work student.   I'm going
to be doing a six-months placement.'

'My name's Sue.   I'm a student nurse.   I'm here for six
weeks.'

'My name's Barbara.   I'm applying for a job and I've come
to spend a day here.'

'Is that the social therapist's job?' someone checked.

And that, to their relief, was that.   No more questions.
The rest of the meeting was taken up with a discussion about
what had happened the night before, in particular about Tony
who had got drunk at a pub, come back to the community and
broken a window.   It appeared that Nick and the woman who
had introduced them were important people here, but it was
unclear exactly what were their positions.   Some people said
nothing during this meeting.   One or two looked very morose
and Barbara wondered if they were patients.   Most were
dressed in casual clothes - jeans seemed to be the rule.
This surprised Sue, who had expected the staff to wear uniforms.

They were puzzled by some of the words they heard used
repeatedly, phrases like 'acting out', 'projecting', 'group
dynamics'.   They had the uncomfortable feeling that people
who were not present were being criticised without the opportunity to defend themselves, which seemed unfair.   It

emerged from what was said that Tony had become fond of one
of the female staff members and had got drunk after she had
refused to go out with him.   Some of the staff said that
this meant he was 'acting out' instead of talking about his
feelings in a group.   Sue thought it was quite understandable not to want to talk about such personal matters in a
group.   Barbara wondered why the girl in question had refused Tony's invitation.   Ian noticed that the girl herself
was saying nothing, just staring into space.

Just before 9 o'clock the meeting ended and everyone got
up to leave.   The three newcomers stood up too, but with no
idea where to go.   They suddenly felt lost and awkward
again.   Nick came up and spoke to them.

'There's a community meeting now followed by a staff feedback meeting at 10.   You'll probably find it a bit confusing to begin with, not knowing who's who.   After the feedback there are various activity groups - you can decide which
one you want to join.   This afternoon you'll each be allocated to one of the therapy groups, and there should be some
time after that for any questions you might have.   Oh,
you'll probably be asked to introduce yourselves in the community meeting.   We'd better go or we'll be late.'

This information was reassuring but it left many questions.   Who was in charge?   What was the purpose of the
meeting they had just been in, and the one they were going
to?   Did everyone sit in meetings the whole day?   Didn't
anyone ever get a chance to talk to anyone on their own?

They entered a large room furnished only with an assort-
ment of soft and hard chairs along each wall.   The middle
was empty except for a worn-looking carpet.   People were
ambling in and taking their seats.   Many of the staff were
sitting at one end of the room.   The residents, or 'members', were dressed like the staff, in jeans and other casual
clothes.   Apart from recognising faces there was no way to
be sure who was a resident and who was a staff member.   The
number of men and women were about equal, and few of the
residents looked older than thirty-five.   There were between
thirty and forty people in the room.

The sheer size of the meeting seemed overwhelming, especially to Sue and Barbara, who had never been in anything like
this before.   Barbara concentrated on how she could make
herself as inconspicuous as possible.   In marked contrast to
the last meeting there was little conversation.   People

entered and sat in silence.   Some held cups of tea or
coffee, most just sat, waiting.

'I suppose we ought to start,' said a young man hesitantly.

They had not seen him before, so they assumed he must be a
resident.   He began by reading out a report about events in
the community during the previous day and night.   Various
names were mentioned.   At one point the report said that a
resident had been late for his work group.   This was inter-
rupted by a gruff voice from somewhere in the room.

'I had a good reason for being late.   I was waiting for
my probation officer, but he never showed up.'

'Let Roger finish reading the report,' said someone.

'Well, I'm always getting picked on in the reports,
they're a load of rubbish.'

'I'm only reading what's written here,' said Roger.

'Arthur always complains,' said a girl.   'At least he
gets written about.   No one ever mentions me.'

'I'd like to hear the rest of the report,' said one of the
staff.   Roger continued reading.   When he had finished
someone asked where were Tony and one or two other absentees.
It was a pity, she said, that Tony had not been here to
listen to what had been read out about him.   Nick then told
the meeting about his conversation with Tony earlier that
morning, and said it seemed as though Tony were set on getting himself kicked out of the community.   Nick suggested
that a member of Tony's small group might be able to persuade
him to come to the meeting.   One of the residents said he
would try, and left the room.

'I think the chairman has forgotten that we have some newcomers with us today,' said a voice from somewhere.   Sue,
Ian and Barbara felt the spotlight turned on them.   Barbara
felt panicky as the other two introduced themselves, but
heard herself do the same in a sort of disembodied voice.
No one asked them any questions after they had introduced
themselves.   In fact, quite the opposite, a deep silence
seemed to descend on the meeting, so suddenly that it might
almost have been at a signal.   Was it something I said,
thought Barbara, who had spoken last.   She wasn't sure what
she had said, such been her state of nervousness.

They've just noticed us, thought Ian, and they don't want us
here.   Perhaps they are going to ask us to leave.   Sue was
feeling quite detached from it all.   She thought it was
rather amusing, all those people waiting for something to
happen.   If they don't have anything more to discuss why
don't they end the meeting, she wondered, but repressed an
urge to smile - someone might ask her what was funny and she
could not possibly tell them.   Cautiously one or two residents began to roll cigarettes.   The silence continued.

'I feel pretty awkward in this silence,' came a voice from
somewhere, 'and I think if I were one of the new arrivals I'd
feel even more awkward.   It seems we don't really want to
welcome them.'

'Oh God, not the spotlight again,' thought Barbara, feeling a bit sick.

'I do feel apprehensive at the moment,' said Ian, glad of
the opportunity to speak.   Barbara could not believe how
brave he was.   Sue was debating whether to ask what the
meeting was for when the resident who had gone out to fetch
Tony returned.   Tony could not be found, and a discussion
immediately began about whether more people should go out to
look for him.   Some were in favour of this but others
thought it would only encourage Tony to carry on acting in
this way.   No agreement could be reached since everyone
seemed to have a different view.   Instead of concentrating
on coming to a decision, the newcomers were puzzled when some
of the staff began to comment on other things.   There was a
remark that Tony was not the only member of the community who
wanted to have a special relationship with one of the staff,
and that some people were using the present situation to
avoid talking about their feelings towards other people in
the room.   This struck the trio as a confusing diversion
from the task in hand - deciding what to do about Tony - and
they had the impression that no one was really in control of
the meeting.   This impression was confirmed when Arthur
repeated his opinion that it was all a load of rubbish and
got up and walked out of the room.   As he did so Tony
appeared.   Someone said it was starting to be like a railway
station.   Everyone laughed and the tension in the room
eased.

'I'm glad you decided to come after all.'

'I wanted to know what people were saying about me.'

The meeting fell into silence again, but not for long.

'I feel pretty pissed off with the way you've been behaving, Tony.   You treat this place like a doss house,' said a resident.

'Why should I care what anyone else feels.   No one cares how I feel.'

'That's not true,' said a girl, 'Sarah cares, or you wouldn't have asked her out.'

'That stupid cow.'

Sarah, who had hardly taken part till now, bit her lip and seemed near to tears.

'If I was Sarah I'd brain you for saying that,' said the girl.

'I think Sarah can speak for herself,' said Nick.

'I'm sorry,' said Sarah, 'I feel quite upset over all this.'   Tears began to roll down her cheeks.   The newcomers were disturbed to see a staff member showing such emotion in front of the residents.   Sue wondered if Sarah would get into trouble for becoming overinvolved, as one of the nurses at her hospital had done.

'I think,' said Nick, 'that it's good Tony should see that people do care, and that he can upset them when he acts the way he does.'

'I thought I could help Tony better by talking on our own,' said Sarah.   'He said he couldn't talk in the groups. When he started telling me lots of things in confidence I found it very difficult, I didn't know what to do.   I wanted to bring it up in the group, but Tony said he would leave the community if I did that.'   She stopped, seemingly at a loss for words.

'I think it's really good that you've been able to bring this into the community meeting,' said one of the staff. Other people nodded sympathetically, and some then spoke of their own difficulties when relationships in the community created divided loyalties between individuals and the community.   The atmosphere in the meeting gradually changed from one of tension and confrontation to one of sharing feelings and problems.

The meeting fell into silence again, but not for long.

'I feel pretty pissed off with the way you've been behaving, Tony.   You treat this place like a doss house,' said a
resident.

'Why should I care what anyone else feels.   No one cares
how I feel.'

'That's not true,' said a girl, 'Sarah cares, or you
wouldn't have asked her out.'

'That stupid cow.'

Sarah, who had hardly taken part till now, bit her lip and
seemed near to tears.

'If I was Sarah I'd brain you for saying that,' said the
girl.

'I think Sarah can speak for herself,' said Nick.

'I'm sorry,' said Sarah, 'I feel quite upset over all
this.'   Tears began to roll down her cheeks.   The newcomers
were disturbed to see a staff member showing such emotion in
front of the residents.   Sue wondered if Sarah would get
into trouble for becoming overinvolved, as one of the nurses
at her hospital had done.

'I think,' said Nick, 'that it's good Tony should see that
people do care, and that he can upset them when he acts the
way he does.'

'I thought I could help Tony better by talking on our
own,' said Sarah.   'He said he couldn't talk in the groups.
When he started telling me lots of things in confidence I
found it very difficult, I didn't know what to do.   I wanted
to bring it up in the group, but Tony said he would leave the
community if I did that.'   She stopped, seemingly at a loss
for words.

'I think it's really good that you've been able to bring
this into the community meeting,' said one of the staff.
Other people nodded sympathetically, and some then spoke of
their own difficulties when relationships in the community
created divided loyalties between individuals and the community.   The atmosphere in the meeting gradually changed from
one of tension and confrontation to one of sharing feelings
and problems.

There was a pause.

'How about you?' someone asked.   Barbara was dreading
this, she had nothing sensible to say.

'I don't really know how I feel at the moment.   There's
so much to take in.'

To her surprise some of the staff nodded sympathetically.
Then someone asked who would be free to see so-and-so's relatives if they came up today and the conversation changed
course again.   The newcomers were left feeling that no clear
guidance or answers to their questions had been given.   It
was a feeling they were to become familiar with.

Following the staff feedback meeting everyone went off to
join different activities.   Sue joined the kitchen group
which was preparing lunch for the community.   After the un-
certainties and elusiveness of the meetings it was a very
welcome change to be engaged in a down to earth, practical
job, with an opportunity to talk to people one at a time.
Barbara joined the art group.   Large sheets of paper were
rolled out on the floor and everyone took part in creating a
large painting with the simple instruction from the art therapist to paint whatever they felt like painting.   In half an
hour they had produced a huge, riotously coloured network of
flowers, faces, trees, squiggles, loops and roads, and then
sat around it talking about what it looked like and how they
had felt while doing it.   Ian joined the cleaning group and
was given the job of cleaning the stains off the doors that
had first caught his eye when they arrived.   Little had he
thought he would become so closely acquainted with them!
Other people in his group were brushing the stairs and tidying the communal rooms.   A paid 'domestic' was vacuum-clean-
ing the carpets because hospital safety regulations did not
permit residents to use electrical appliances - a source of
continuing conflict between the community and its parent hospital, a resident told Ian.

At 12 o'clock they had lunch with the residents.   Some of
the staff also ate with the residents while others went off
to the canteen of the main hospital.   It was noticeable that
some residents seemed eager to ask them questions while
others ignored them.   They were asked why they had come,
what they were studying and what they thought of the community.   They learned that most residents had been there
between three and twelve months, and that while some liked it
others were unhappy and talked of leaving.   One or two of

the dissatisfied residents seemed to take the opportunity to
unburden themselves to the newcomers, telling them of the
strict rules, the boredom, the feeling that they weren't getting anywhere.   One girl asked Barbara if she knew of any
other therapeutic community she could go to, but Barbara
didn't know.

After lunch they each joined one of the small groups.
These met on three afternoons a week for an hour and a half.
Each group had about ten residents and three or four staff
members.   They sat round in a circle in fairly comfortable
but worn armchairs.   Here again, as in the morning community
meeting, they felt rather like intruders.   More so in a way,
because more intimate and personal things were talked about.
Residents spoke about their feelings towards one another, and
about things that had happened to them outside.   There were
also quite long silences which seemed more relaxed than in
the large morning meeting, and with fewer people there also
seemed to be more expectation that the newcomers would take
part.   They noticed that the staff often took the lead in
steering the discussion, asking questions or bringing in
silent members.   Ian, who had read about therapeutic communities, was surprised that the staff did not say much about
their own feelings or experience.

After the groups had finished the residents went to have
tea and the staff stayed behind to talk briefly about what
had happened in the group.   Then it was time for the
promised question and answer session - complete with a welcome pot of tea.

They were back in the room they had started in at 8.30 -
the green room.   That seemed a very long time ago.   One,
two, three, four, five, six meetings ago, counted Ian.   They
began to realise how tired they felt.   It had been an exhausting day although they had spent most of it sitting down.
They were joined by Nick and Sarah, and by Roger, the resident chairman in the community meeting.   Nick told them that
Jean (the middle-aged lady who had appeared to be one of the
leaders in the staff meetings) couldn't come and sent her
apologies.   He had hoped that more staff would have come but
it was always difficult to get people to go to things they
didn't have to, especially at this time of day.

'I'm not surprised,' said Sue, 'I'm exhausted.'

'Do you mean the staff feel the same way as the residents
do?' asked Ian.

'How do you mean?' asked Nick.

'Some of the residents were saying at lunchtime and in the small group that they didn't like being here or having to go to all the group meetings.   And there was Tony this morning.'

'Yes, well I suppose we all feel that way from time to time.   It's not an easy place to work.'

'What I wanted to ask,' said Sue, 'was why none of the staff introduced themselves when we were asked to.   I still don't know who anyone is or what anyone does.'

Nick nodded slowly.   'Yes, I suppose it's difficult to know where to begin.   I mean, everybody introducing themselves, you wouldn't have remembered.'

'What do you do?' Ian asked directly.

'Well, my title is "charge nurse" but that doesn't really tell you what I do.   I mean I don't go around giving people pills and injections.'

'What is your role then?'

'Basically it involves being a member of the community, taking part in meetings, doing things with residents like cleaning dishes and playing table tennis, then at other times standing back and trying to understand what's going on, like why somebody walks out of a meeting or gets upset over something.   Sometimes I act as a facilitator - in my small group - helping residents talk about their feelings.   But often other residents are better at doing that than I am.   I think an important part of my job is being around as a support, for staff as well as residents.'

'What roles do other staff take?' asked Barbara.

'There isn't a clear distinction between the roles differ-ent staff take.   Although we each have different profession-al backgrounds a lot depends on the personality and experi-ence of the individuals.'

'But there must be some hierarchy,' said Sue, 'after all, it is a hospital.'

'Yes, but not the kind of hospital you're used to,' replied Nick, a bit sharply Sue thought.   'Here the hierar-

chy is a lot flatter.   People don't tell others what to do,
decisions are discussed by everyone who's affected.   I
trained in a general hospital and I can tell you it's a lot
different.'

'But at the end of the day isn't it the doctors who are in
charge?'

'There may be times when one of the doctors takes the lead,
but there are other times when I or one of the other staff
take the lead.   There isn't just one leader.'

'I know everyone is supposed to be equal and all that,'
said Ian, 'but I get the feeling that there are some hidden
rules that no one admits to.'

'How do you mean?'

'Well, for example, it seemed to me that only certain
staff were allowed to give their views in the staff meeting,
and that staff came to the rescue of another staff member in
the community meeting.'

'You mean Sarah this morning?' asked Nick.

'I think it can seem like that.'   Sarah spoke for the
first time.   'I remember feeling the same way when I first
arrived, three months ago.   No one would explain anything,
you just had to work it out for yourself.'

'Wouldn't it be possible to give everyone a handout when
they came,' asked Sue, 'explaining how the unit works?'

'We tried that once but it didn't seem to make much difference,' answered Nick.   'People still felt the same way.'

'There is a handout,' Roger corrected Nick, 'only we've
run out of copies.'

'I didn't mind about not knowing people's names,' said
Barbara, 'but I thought some of the groups were really difficult to take part in.   I found it easier to talk to people
over lunch and in the art session this morning.'

'I still don't know what the purpose of the meetings is,'
added Sue.   'If the aim is to get residents to talk about
their problems surely it would be better if they met a staff
member individually.   I don't think I would want to talk
about my problems in front of a whole lot of people.'

'Why not?' asked Nick.

'I'd want to choose who I talked to.'

'I know what you mean,' Roger, the chairman of the community meeting, joined in the conversation. 'When I first
came here I was terrified of the large groups - afraid to
fidget or cough or do anything to attract attention.   It
wasn't much better in the small groups - there were only two
or three people in the community I felt I trusted, and none
of them were in my group.   I thought, "if I say anything
they'll use it against me."   It took a long time before I
began to feel that I was one of the community, that people
actually cared about me.'

'How did that change happen?' asked Barbara.

'I think it was when I wasn't the newest member any more,
you know, the baby.   When other people came and I saw them
feeling the way I had, then I thought, well I'm part of this
community, I can help them.'

'Yes, I think I feel that talking to you,' Sarah said to
the newcomers.   'I remember feeling that I couldn't say anything in the meetings.   I still feel that sometimes.'

'How did you feel being the centre of attention in the
community meeting?' asked Ian.   'I mean, I sort of wondered
if you were putting it on for effect.'

'Oh, I don't agree,' said Barbara, 'I thought it must have
been really hard for her.'

'Well,' said Ian, 'it seemed such a good demonstration,
you know, "This is how a therapeutic community works".'

'That's like your feelings that there are hidden rules,
some behind-the-scenes manipulation,' said Nick.

Ian nodded, but felt uncomfortable having what he said
commented on in this way.

'It took me a long time to pluck up the courage to say
something,' said Sarah, 'but when I did it wasn't so bad.   I
think when you first come you're terribly afraid of saying
the wrong thing, but after a while you begin to realise that
there isn't really a right or wrong thing, and you just have
to be yourself.'

'That's what worried me,' said Barbara.   'In the small group this afternoon, I kept trying to think of something to say, but by the time I could think of something people were talking about something different.   So in the end, I didn't say anything.'

'I felt more like an observer,' said Sue, 'so it was all right to sit back and not say anything.   I think that might change, if I get to know the residents a bit more.'

'Yes,' said Barbara, 'there was a feeling that the staff had it all worked out and if you said anything you might upset what they were trying to do.'

'It seems you all had a similar feeling,' said Nick, 'of being outsiders, not sure how to fit in or what part to play.'

They all nodded in agreement.   Ian was feeling annoyed. He felt that they, in particular he himself, were being ana- lysed by Nick.   It's all very well for you, he thought, sit- ting back and watching us grope around and make fools of our- selves.   But he couldn't actually say this.   What he did say was,

'Do any of the staff leave because they feel they don't fit in?'   It was Sarah who answered.

'Someone left about a month ago.   She was the next staff member to arrive after me.   She was very spontaneous and I think she felt too restricted by all the meetings and the daily structure.'

'Don't you feel restricted?' Ian asked.

'Yes, I do, sometimes.   But I think it's more to do with my wanting someone to tell me what to do, being afraid to stick my neck out in case I get laughed at or criticised.'

Barbara felt both sympathetic and impressed listening to Sarah.   It was just what she often felt, not only today but in lots of situations, but she wouldn't have been able to put it into words that clearly.

There was a pause.   Nick looked at his watch.   He said he had another meeting to go to and they probably wanted to get away and mull over their impressions of the day. Barbara would be contacted as soon as the staff had had a chance to discuss her application.   There would be another,

more formal, interview.   And with that the meeting, and
their first day, were over.

    Travelling home, each was conscious of an element of sur-
prise in what they had experienced.   Sue had not looked forward to coming to Alexander House - doing psychiatry had
seemed a bit of a chore.   She would have been content to
observe things passively and wait for the time to pass.
Instead she had been surprised at how interesting she had
found it.   Admittedly some of the staff seemed rather
strange, with their peculiar jargon and search for hidden
meanings in ordinary things.   But what people talked about -
what residents talked about - seemed much more real than she
had anticipated from reading books and going to lectures on
psychiatry.   They got upset over the sorts of things that
would upset her, like being ignored or made to do things you
didn't want to.   The atmosphere was a lot more open than on
general hospital wards - a student who cried in front of
patients would probably be sent home or transferred to
another ward - and the staff were able to disagree with each
other in a way that she had never seen before.   Ian might be
right about things going on 'behind the scenes', but you
wouldn't expect to know everything on your first day.

    Ian was experiencing a rather different state of surprise.
He had expected the day to be enjoyable and stimulating, but
now he found himself feeling confused and annoyed.   The
staff were not as spontaneous as they pretended they were.
The things they said sounded rather 'pat' and automatic and
Nick had been evasive in his answers, ending the meeting to
avoid being challenged.   Obviously he, Ian, was too percep-
tive for the staff's liking.   Rather than risk having more
questions turned back on him he decided that for the rest of
the week he wouldn't say anything, just stay quiet and
observe as Sue had done.

    Barbara had expected a therapeutic community to be a
friendly, informal place, with little distinction between
staff and residents, everyone taking part in an equal way.
She had been surprised at the amount of organisation and formality.   Different groups at different times for different
purposes, different people taking different roles - it all
seemed artificial.   The natural, easy-going interactions she
had imagined did occur, but only in the art group and at
lunchtime.   She had begun to feel during the day that it was
quite beyond her to understand, let alone play a useful part
in all these activities.   Then hearing Sarah talking gave
her hope; the staff were not all so different from her, in

time she might also be able to express herself like that.
Perhaps they wouldn't offer her the job anyway.   But if they
did - would she take it?   It gave her butterflies inside to
think about that.

Chapter 9
Some do's and don'ts for beginners in a therapeutic community

The narrative in Chapter 8 may have given you some impression of what joining a therapeutic community is like, and some idea of what to expect (and not to expect) about your own role in the community. It may be useful in addition to have a few dos and don'ts as a general guide in the first weeks. These weeks will amost certainly be difficult ones, as you try to find or create a place for yourself that suits both you and the community. This process may be eased if you bear in mind the following points.

Do look on this as an opportunity to learn about yourself as well as others: whatever your professional reason for entering a therapeutic community it will also have a tremendous personal impact. Be prepared for this and take it as an opportunity to learn about your own feelings and responses, as well as about other people and their problems.

Don't expect to be told exactly what to do: if you are a student or trainee you may be used to receiving instructions about what you are expected to do. In a therapeutic community you are more likely to be given a brief welcome (not even that sometimes) and left to get on with things and find your own personal place, so -

Do talk to people: introduce yourself, let people know who you are and why you have come. There is no hierarchy of the type where those at the bottom must only speak if they are spoken to so you need not worry about speaking out of turn.* At first you may not always know if the person you

* In concept-based therapeutic communities there are certain formalities about relations between residents at different levels in the hierarchy (see Chapter 5).

126

are speaking to is a resident or staff member, or what senio-
rity they have in the community. This doesn't matter - get
to know people as individuals. You will soon start to know
who is who in the community by the roles they take in the
various activities and meetings.

Do get involved in what is going on: take whatever opportunities present themselves for taking part in the life of
the community. These may include jobs like cleaning and
tidying, preparing food, sharing meals with residents, taking
part in games and recreational activities, simply talking to
people, and participating in the various group meetings.

Do be yourself: in a therapeutic community it is all
right to be as you are - shy or outgoing, easy-going or critical, tense or relaxed. Don't feel you have to pretend to
be someone else, different from the way you are when you are
not at work.

Do say what you actually feel: by saying what you really
think and feel you will let the other members of the community get to know you and you will start to feel part of the
community. If you hold back from saying what you feel you
are likely to remain feeling on the 'outside'.

Don't hold back for fear of saying the wrong thing: newcomers often worry about saying the wrong thing and upsetting
someone. People do get upset or angry at times, but learning to cope with such feelings is one of the aims of a therapeutic community so there is no need to prevent this happening. Sometimes this means letting other people express
their feelings even if it makes you feel bad or guilty. And
the other staff or residents will be able to support someone
who is upset so you need not feel 'on your own'. Newcomers
also often assume that the staff have carefully laid plans
for running meetings which the beginner might accidentally
muck up. In practice there are seldom plans which are as
specific as the newcomer imagines. Indeed if there were
such plans worked out in advance by some of the staff, then
the community would fail in its aim of getting every member -
including you - to share in the responsibility for what goes
on in the community.

Don't feel you have to produce 'pearls of wisdom': ordinary, everyday statements are as helpful as clever interpretations or wise advice. In group meetings, especially large
ones, it is easy to imagine that because so many people are
listening anything you say must sound brilliant. In prac-

tice such efforts often reduce participation and make the
atmosphere more tense.   Ordinary expressions of interest or
personal experience tend to make it more comfortable and
intimate.   Your own experience of hearing other people talk
will confirm this.

Don't be put off if you don't get an answer: it can be
unnerving when you say something in a meeting and no one res-
ponds, or someone changes the subject.   All sort of thoughts
crowd in: I've said the wrong thing; they disapprove; they
don't care.... Actually you have been heard, but in a group
which follows a process of free discussion themes get taken
up and dropped according to the current preoccupations of the
group members.   It's not like an ordinary conversation
(although these may occur).   What one person says may get
taken up straight away by someone else, may be returned to
later, or may be taken away and thought about by someone.

It can also be frustrating when you make what you think is
a useful suggestion to be told it wouldn't work, it has
already been tried, or that you don't understand things yet.
It may seem that these responses are simply defending the
status quo, that the staff are unwilling to listen to new
ideas.   This may be true, but maybe a newcomer is reacting
to his or her own experience of becoming a member of the community.   This needs to be worked out - with others if necessary.

A final do - do take things as they come: you will probably get most out of the first few weeks of starting to work
in a therapeutic community if you are not in a rush to
establish a therapeutic role for yourself or to understand
the reason behind everything.   Allow yourself to experience
what it is like not to know, what it is like being new, getting to know the people, voicing your own first impressions
and listening to other people's, participating in activities
and being yourself.   What at first seemed to be a frustrating lack of structure and guidance will become a rewarding
opportunity to learn in a very direct way about personal relationships, healthy and disturbed, and the ways in which
they can be understood and changed.

Chapter 10
Questions of training

(written in collaboration with Jeff Roberts)

The question of what sort of training is generally appropriate for therapeutic community staff has barely begun to be
asked, let alone answered.   Recent practice has varied
widely, from settings in which no special training or experience is required to those in which the staff participate in a
variety of internal and external training programmes and
undertake a personal experience of therapy.   Different
levels of expectation about training are not surprising when
we consider the diversity of origins from which therapeutic
communities have arisen.

Institutional therapeutic communities were created in
order to enhance the work and the morale of staff who had no
training beyond that which qualified them to work in the
institution.   This is not to say that such staff may not go
on to seek further training and experience, but this is
seldom an expectation of the institution.   The small, specialised communities of the democratic-analytic type usually
do expect staff to pursue further training, although they can
do this in a number of ways.   Some communities offer their
new staff an organised programme of supervision, seminars and
support groups while others expect staff to obtain their
training through participation in outside courses.   Where an
independent organisation runs a number of communities, it
may, like the Richmond Fellowship, offer a career structure
linked to its own organised training programme.

Training in concept-based therapeutic communities is, for
ex-addict staff, primarily the experience of going through
such a community as a resident.   For professional staff too,
participation as a resident may be an important part of
training.   These communities also usually have their own
career structure which enables them to employ and promote

129

people who have no formal professional training, as is often
the case for ex-addict staff.   The notion of training is
difficult to ascribe to those communities loosely collected
under the heading of alternative asylum.   Communities for
the handicapped often accept people as 'co-workers' who live
as permanent members of the community.   In other cases the
work may be seen as a period of experience 'en route' to more
specialised professional or therapeutic work, or as an
adjunct to training in psychotherapy.

With such a varied pattern of training options and expectations, you may wonder how to decide about your own training.   In this chapter we will try to deal with a number of
questions which will concern the person who is either working
in a therapeutic community and wishing to increase their
skill and understanding, or considering the possibility of
doing so and wondering whether qualifications or training
would help.   We will look at these issues in terms of four
questions: (1) Do I need a professional qualification?
(2) Do I need any further training?   (3) What do I need to
learn?   (4) What are the resources for training and learning?

DO I NEED A PROFESSIONAL QUALIFICATION?

This can be answered in terms of the advantages and disadvantages of professional qualifications and the training that
precedes them.

Advantages

There is at present no generally recognised qualification
for people who work in therapeutic communities.   This means
that someone wanting to work as a staff member has either to
qualify first in one of the recognised helping professions,
or to work in one of those communities which has its own
career structure and system of staff training.   It is also
possible in some communities to work for a limited time as a
'social therapist' (or in a similar role) as a preliminary to
further professional training.   The first advantage of a
professional qualification, therefore, is that it enables you
to be employed in an institutional setting on a permanent
basis, and provides you with a recognised role within that
institution.   There may be restrictions attached to this
role, but there is also greater security of employment -
important in these times of high unemployment.   It also pro-

vides a supportive kinship with those in the same profession,
who share the same perspective and interests.

A second advantage is that the qualified professional
possesses specific knowledge and skills which can make a
special contribution to the therapeutic community.   The doctor's knowledge of psychiatric symptoms, the teacher's knowledge of children's developing capacities, the occupational
therapist's knowledge of work activities and games can all be
valuable resources in a community.   Therapeutic communities
in many settings are intended to enhance, not replace, individual skills.   Even where they offer a distinct alternative
to prevailing professional ideas on care and treatment, as in
the case of the 'anti-psychiatry' communities, it may be
important for someone to be able to make an informed decision
- for example, deciding if someone's physical condition requires medical treatment.

Third, and in some ways most important, professional
training is good for instilling a sense of the possible, of
what can and cannot be achieved, of the limitations of one's
skills and knowledge.   This is something that therapists
without any professional training (and occasionally those
with) are prone to ignore.   The existence of various therapeutic 'cults' promising a cure for all ills and unhappiness
bears witness to a lack of such realism.   The trained social
worker knows how difficult it is to make the correct decision
about whether to leave a child with its potentially violent
parents or remove the child to a place of safety.   A psychiatrist knows that he cannot read people's minds and is largely reliant on what people are prepared to tell him.   In both
cases the untrained person sometimes has an unrealistic idea
of the possibility of knowing things about other people.
Professional training makes us aware of the limitations of
what we can know or predict and of what we can do to help or
change people.

Disadvantages

So far we have considered what a training in one of the recognised professions is good for.   What is it bad for?   One
disadvantage, or at least a risk, is that qualifications are
seen as a way of achieving superiority over others, or at
least overcoming doubts about one's own adequacy.   An anec-
dote can illustrate this point.

A group of students newly arrived at college were talking

together, imagining what life would be like when they had graduated. They pictured a future scene: some people sitting round a table arguing over an important issue of the day, among them the new graduate. At a key moment in the discussion he plays his ace: he casually remarks that he has a degree. The effect is instantaneous and dramatic. Opposing views are silenced. His own are at once deferred to as the product of greater knowledge and understanding. His superior wisdom is recognised.

Such, at any rate, was these students' daydream. Many of us probably have had such gratifying fantasies from time to time. In part they reflect the quite appropriate desire to have our accomplishments recognised by others, but they may also reflect earlier skirmishes with the unequal world of parents and siblings, teachers and classmates, when we longed for some power that could turn the tables and give us the upper hand. Such feelings contribute to the mystique that qualifications possess. Becoming 'qualified' helps us to achieve not just a useful set of skills and knowledge, but also the kind of self-image we want of being confident, competent, accepted, respected. Qualifications do confer status, and status does bolster our confidence, but they should also leave plenty of room for continuing doubts and questions. This is not an argument against becoming qualified in one of the helping professions, only against the idea that a qualification can or should rescue its possessor from vulnerability.

A second and more important problem is that professional training tends to create a narrow view of one's role. The same perspective which those in one profession share and which provides a sense of identity, also militates against the sharing and blurring of roles between disciplines that is an essential feature of therapeutic communities. In a traditional psychiatric hospital each profession concerns itself with a different aspect of the patient's treatment. The doctor diagnoses illness and prescribes treatment; the nurse observes, comforts and controls the patient; the occupational therapist provides remedial work experience; the social worker deals with the home situation; the psychologist assesses the patient's personality, and so on. Members of each discipline recognise the contribution of the others, but seldom fully appreciate their points of view, and almost never take over their roles.

Professionals accustomed to this way of working may find it difficult and strange to take a broader view of their

work, to operate in terms of diagnosis and control and work
and the family situation and the patient's personality all at
the same time, although this of course is what the patient
has to contend with.   Still less would they feel comfortable
in sharing their decision-making with the patients.   Indeed,
what is deemed proper therapeutic practice in a therapeutic
community may be experienced as bad practice or even unethi-
cal by highly trained professionals.   A trained nurse may
become extremely uncomfortable if events she and her colleagues observe are not directly acted upon by medical staff.
She may find it hard to understand that she is expected to
respond to a situation rather than merely observe and report
it.   In a similar way, a doctor will feel guilty if unable
to respond in a conventional medical manner to a situation;
for example by making decisions, giving individual attention
and prescribing medication.

These expectations are not a matter only of professional
training.   A study of nurses and doctors with different
orientations towards psychiatric treatment has shown that
their attitudes to staff-patient relationships and staff control are related to more general attitudes.   For example,
staff with a traditional medical orientation were found to
hold more conservative views concerning authority and to have
more practical, factual interests.   Those who subscribed to
therapeutic community principles tended to be more interested
in ideas and emotional problems and to hold more liberal or
'anarchist' attitudes towards authority. (1)   It seems
likely that such attitudes play an important part in many
people's choice of a professional orientation.   While some
choose to work in a therapeutic community, and others are
ready to unlearn professional training that did not suit
them, some qualified staff may not be suited to this style of
work because of the combination of their previous training
and their interests and attitudes.

DO I NEED ANY FURTHER TRAINING?

If you are already qualified in one of the helping professions, or are hoping to be, you may wonder if you need to
know anything more to work in a therapeutic community.   You
may already feel that you know a lot about people and how to
help them.   If you have chosen to work in a psycho-therapeu-
tic field it is likely that you are also aware of a special
ability you have, of being able to get closely in touch with
the thoughts and feelings of other people.   You are keen to
get started and, with some justification, feel that you need

no further knowledge, particularly in any academic sense.
Indeed with long nights of studying facts and figures and the
painful experience of examinations in your recent past, you
could have quite an aversion to more learning.   Given a few
years' experience you expect that the raw materials of
talent, enthusiasm and prior training will fit nicely into
place, that you will become a good enough staff member.
Many people share this point of view and there are strong
arguments for it.   Others, however, would argue that in
order to achieve the goal of being a good enough staff member
it is necessary to learn in an organised way, what therapeutic communities are and how best to participate in them.   We
will present arguments for both points of view.   This we
hope will enable you to decide whether you believe training
for therapeutic community work is necessary and, more impor-
tantly, whether it is necessary for you.

'Training is not necessary'

The egalitarian ideal of many therapeutic communities implies
that no member of a community is given more importance than
any other.   Requiring no more than their essential humanity,
everyone with natural ability can be a therapist without
further training.   The natural therapeutic abilities of the
staff members of a therapeutic community will be elicited by
leaders of the staff group and constrained by the formal
rules of the organisation.   Thus staff members are encouraged to express themselves as freely and honestly as possible
and to develop to the full any special talents they may have.
At the same time, they are expected to attend community and
staff groups regularly, to be responsible and empathic in
their confrontations and to avoid developing such relationships with colleagues or clients as will undermine the group
ethos or culture.   Given this context each staff member may
then be expected to produce an optimum performance without
further formal training.

   The flexibility and enthusiasm of youth is particularly
valued.   It was with this in mind that Maxwell Jones first
introduced 'social therapists' into the Henderson hospital.
These young people, more often women than men, usually in the
year before taking up a degree course or other training,
would be offered 12 months' work in the therapeutic community.   They were (and still are) seen as an important element in the therapeutic functioning of this and other units.
Such a process of short-term involvement protects these
staff members from becoming stale or overstressed.   Were

they to stay longer, staleness would rob their work of its
creativity, and they might suffer from the ill-effects of
prolonged emotional involvement in an intense and often
stressful situation.

Another reason why training may not be useful is that the
therapeutic community approach is not widely applied within
the health services.   There are therefore only limited
career opportunities available for people skilled in therapeutic community work, and the skills required for working in
a therapeutic community are not acknowledged in the way
health services are organised.   Indeed, if there were a
relevant career structure it would need to be cross-discipli-
nary.   Such a structure would be immensely difficult to
create in the face of professional rivalries and official
bureaucracy.   At present then, there is nothing tangible to
train for, since most people after a brief period in a therapeutic community return to a more conventional setting to
continue their work.   Indeed, those who remain in therapeutic community work as long-term senior practitioners or
leaders of communities, often function quite adequately without having had any formalised training.

If there are no special skills required, and most people
are encouraged to remain only briefly in the work, it would
be pointless to impose on them the rigours of additional
training.   Having worked hard to achieve a professional
qualification, it is reasonable to leave studying behind.
You are an expert in a particular field and should be treated
as such.   You should be able to settle down to enjoy the
fruits of earlier labours and not have to expend time, energy
and hard-earned money on further training.

'Training is necessary'

Therapeutic communities are hard to establish and keep going.
Some therapeutic communities have short lives and others
scarcely get off the ground.   On the other hand, mental hospitals and other institutions seem to go on forever.   One of
the difficulties in establishing and maintaining therapeutic
communities is that they are subject to episodes of destructive behaviour.   These can be damaging to the organisation
and may even lead to the closure of the community itself.
Such episodes can occur periodically as part of a cycle of
oscillation in a community.   Training is necessary if staff
are to learn to understand and deal with such behaviour, or
at least not to participate in it or aggravate it.

Destructive behaviour refers here to those acts which are not acceptable to the staff as a whole and are not controllable by the rules and sanctions of the organisations.   This can include drunkenness, violence to property or individuals, sexual behaviour and drug taking.   Such behaviour may escalate until one or more individuals, identified as the ringleaders, are discharged and the community recovers from a state of shock, slowly to become therapeutic again.   It can be argued that such events are intrinsic to therapeutic communities and unavoidable.   However, closer observation often suggests that staff may provoke, maintain or otherwise contribute to them.

In one therapeutic community there was a threat of closure because of the government's financial cuts.   At the height of this threat the staff, angry and exhausted in their attempts to save the community, went along with a community decision to accept an individual with a long criminal record.   Shortly afterwards a large sum of money was stolen, the new member being the most likely culprit. It had been the staff's duty to supervise the money kept in the community, but it had been left too readily available.   In doing this the staff were indirectly helping an attack on the very community they were striving to keep open.

In another community, it was extremely difficult to persuade clients to stick to a rule of no alcohol in the lunch period.   Only when staff gave up their Friday lunch-time pub visits and ended having their own parties for departing members did it become possible to encourage (without hypocrisy) the enforcing of this rule.

On both occasions staff members were participating in destructive processes and tending to blame administrators and clients for the results.   With greater intellectual and emotional awareness of their part in these processes, the staff might have been able to recognise and avoid participating in them.

Staff members are human beings and every human being has difficulty with some aspects of his or her emotional life. Working in a therapeutic community will sooner or later bring each staff member face-to-face with these difficulties.   On such occasions a number of reactions may occur.

1 Staff members may deny such difficulties and (unconsciously) identifying similar problems in a client may

project their own problems into that client.   To take a
hypothetical example, a basically heterosexual staff
member and a basically heterosexual client may both have
some homosexual feelings which they find difficult to
acknowledge.   In order not to face his or her own feelings the staff member may 'project' these on to the
client, and see the client as someone with a major problem
over homosexuality.

2   The staff member may choose a defensive and rigid way
of relating to patients who provoke the re-experiencing of
personal difficulties.

3   The staff member may experience, or be put at risk of,
some form of breakdown.

4   He or she may make an impulsive decision to leave the
community.

Appropriate training which helps staff members to be aware
of and accept their own problems and life experience will
reduce the likelihood of dealing with them in one of these
ways.

Staff members may also misunderstand the therapeutic process and conduct relationships with clients and the community
on the basis of their own ideas about therapy and their own
personal philosophy of life.   This may at times be helpful,
but can result in giving inappropriate advice and attempting
to coerce clients into following a path dictated by the goals
and values of the therapist.

'Burn out' is a problem which is becoming increasingly
recognised among people working in the caring professions.
This term refers to the state of staleness and emotional
upset which happens all too often to members of the caring
professions, usually relative early in their career, and
which produces disillusionment and defensiveness in the place
of enthusiasm and optimism.   Two important factors can lead
to 'burn out'.   The first is the inevitable and repeated
disappointment resulting from clients' progress not coming up
to expectations.   The second is the way in which members of
the helping professions tend to work excessively long hours
with too little time and energy devoted to developing their
own lives.   This is particularly true in therapeutic communities, which provide an exciting career but are not meant to
offer their staff members a total way of life.

'Burn out' is less of a problem for the short-term staff
member, yet it might be argued that the repeated loss of
short-term staff, whether through pre-planning or as a result
of disillusioned drop-outs, is a waste of talent and partial-
ly gathered experience. Indeed, if the short-term staff
member makes no attempt to learn from his or her experiences,
and is offered no special opportunities to do this, very
little may be gained from them. For longer-term 'permanent'
staff members, however, the problem of 'burn out' may threat-
en both career and well-being. Those who are well informed
about therapeutic communities generally and about the expectations attached to their own role in their own community
are, we think, less susceptible to 'burn out' than those who
have had no therapeutic community training. There are, of
course, people who have worked in therapeutic communities for
years and are not 'burnt out', or have apparently suffered no
ill-effects. Some of these have no doubt devised their own
training scheme, while others may be the survivors at the end
point of a process of natural selection, although they will
no doubt have gone through many difficult and painful times.

If the avoidance of destructive behaviour, defensive reactions and 'burn out' appear to be negative reasons for training, the positive side is the potential for a more rewarding
career in a therapeutic community. This applies not only in
professional terms but in personal ones too. Therapeutic
communities have as one of their goals that members should
understand the meaning of what is happening to them in their
lives and in the therapeutic community itself. Proper
training can give people the tools to explore and understand
both themselves and therapeutic communities more fully.
This will increase the feeling of life in a therapeutic community as an exciting and meaningful unfolding of events
rather than a ritualised, incomprehensive and often painful
daily grind.

One further argument for training concerns not the individuals who work in them but the survival of therapeutic
communities themselves. The enlightened era of moral treatment disappeared partly because its advocates could not
reconcile themselves to the need for professional training.
They held the view, advanced in our arguments against training, that personal qualities were all that counted. In the
event this meant that communities died when their leaders
died or retired. Today a failure to develop appropriate
training programmes may have the same results: communities
which are dependent on the skills and dedication of a few
enthusiastic individuals. Such communities can survive a

long time, but will run into difficulties when the leader
leaves or dies.   There is also the situation where a therapeutic community enterprise fails to get off the ground.
Rather than blame the approach itself, we would argue that
such failures often arise through a lack of staff who both
believe in and understand the methods they are hoping to put
into practice.   Enthusiasm allied to skill and understanding
is the combination most likely to ensure the continued development of therapeutic communities.

WHAT DO I NEED TO LEARN?

What should the aims of training be?   What kinds of skills
and understanding are needed in a therapeutic community?
One way to answer this is to discover what people who actually work in therapeutic communities see as their main training
needs.   We have gathered information on this in the following way.   Thirty-six staff members from many different communities applied to participate in two residential training
weekends, entitled 'Learning from Experience in Therapeutic
Community Living', organised in England by the Association of
Therapeutic Communities.   Prior to coming they were asked
what three things they most hoped to gain from the experience.   We have summarised their answers into five general
categories, and elaborated some of these in order to bring
out their relevance for therapeutic community work.

   'Knowledge about therapeutic communities' and particular
aspects of therapy.   This was the type of learning requested
most often.   Applicants wanted to know and understand the
ideas and concepts involved in therapeutic community work.
This need was expressed in two ways, reflecting different
levels of experience and involvement.   The first was a need
for a general orientation, a wish to know from the outside as
it were: 'How do they work?'   'What are the different concepts?'   The second was more specific, related to various
aspects of working in a therapeutic community.   For example,
they wanted to know, 'the place of control for a worker in a
therapeutic community', 'the benefits and difficulties of
role-blurring for staff', and 'how members learn from each
other, how learning is directed, or rather facilitated'.
This is knowledge needed by people doing a job who feel mud-
dled or uncertain about their own or others' roles and want
to clarify their thinking.   The quotations suggest that a
dilemma faced by therapeutic community workers is trying to
put into practice such goals as equality and shared responsibility in the face of pressures (either from others or from

within themselves) to take control, to organise and tell
others what to do.

Linked to a wish for knowledge, some staff were seeking
'increased professional skills and effectiveness'.   One
wanted to 'learn certain techniques which would be of use in
dealing with resistant subjects', another, 'to balance activity against pure rushing about', and a third, 'to become more
sensitive to the group process'.

Different kinds of skill are implied here.   The first
person asks for 'techniques' for 'dealing with' other people
called 'subjects'.   A difficulty is implied in the way the
statement is phrased.   If techniques are used as the 'basis'
for relating to a person, whether they be kind or harsh techniques, the relationship is not likely to be on in which
human qualities can flourish.   One needs first to see the
other as a person and to make a relationship with that other
person.   Once a relationship is established certain techniques may then be helpful - for example the use of confrontation, interpretation, humour, contracts, and so on are all
useful therapeutic techniques.   Because they occur in the
context of a relationship between two or more people, such
techniques cannot easily be taught away from that context,
and they are often best learnt in living situations - a therapeutic community, a therapy group, an experiential group,
personal therapy.

The person who wants to 'balance activity against pure
rushing about' recognises an important distinction.   What is
being sought is the ability to stop, think and plan rather
than get carried away by repeated demands for action.   Re-
sisting such pressures can be very difficult, especially for
someone who has a practical orientation.   The ability to
combine action and reflection, doing and deliberation, is a
skill peculiarly important in therapeutic communities, where
excesses of both can flourish, and where members may get
'typecast' as either 'doers' or 'deliberators', making it
hard to combine and balance the two.

The third quotation concerns a fundamental area of learning for anyone who wants to use groups as a therapeutic
medium.   Group process refers to those phenomena which are
characteristic of unstructured groups, and which affect all
the members of the group.   These include pressures to conform, reactions to leadership, scapegoating, etc.   The therapeutic community worker also needs to be aware of the different kinds of process that go on in small and large groups.

Without this awareness, the staff member is likely to attri-
bute what he sees to individuals: e.g. Kathy is tired, John
is being provocative, and so on.   Awareness of group process
reveals the less visible side of behaviour, the existence of
patterns and pressures which affect a group or community as a
whole.

These different needs for increased skill include both
'external', practical skills and 'internal', awareness
skills.   Techniques we learn from watching and copying
others; sensitivity requires us to attune ourselves to what
goes on within us.   Therapeutic communities need both kinds
of skills.

A third kind of learning staff members want is to 'learn
about oneself'.   They want to learn about their relationships with others, to learn how they appear to others, to
explore themselves in a group situation.   In some cases
there are particular questions, such as 'Do I have a contribution to make towards therapeutic community living?' and
'How will I cope with the pressure and power of the therapeutic community as a member rather than as the staff?'   Self-
learning may be sought in the interests of being a better
staff member.   It may also, quite justifiably, be sought for
the sake of the learner.   If you are attracted to the idea
of helping other people understand themselves better because
you also want to understand yourself better, there is no
reason why you should not pursue both goals.

How can learning about yourself make you a better staff
member?   One way is by increasing your empathic understanding of others.   Being able to look at another person's
world through their eyes requires not that you have had
exactly the same experience as the other person, but that you
have experienced similar kinds of thoughts, feelings, and reactions.   Often we are working with people whose feelings
are extremely painful.   No one enjoys painful feelings and,
if we can, we push them out of awareness.   Becoming more
self-aware means being able to acknowledge and face these
feelings in ourselves.   If we can do this, we can then begin
to respond to others with genuine empathy rather than simply
with kindness and consolation.   We also become aware of the
reluctance in ourselves to acknowledge all our feelings, and
this may make us less impatient or angry when others appear
to resist our best efforts.

A second way in which self-awareness helps is in revealing
to us biases and blindspots which often hinder work with par-

ticular clients.   When someone evokes a strong feeling reaction - whether positive or negative - it becomes difficult
to think clearly about our relationship with that person.
Self-awareness can help us to check the impulse to use such a
feeling as sufficient justification for action.   For
example, if a woman habitually makes others reject her, it
may be more useful to try to understand how and why she does
this rather than simply to repeat the pattern.

Another aspect of self-awareness is learning the effect we
have on others.   This is looking at the situation from the
point of view of the person who gets rejected.   If she can
see what it is that she does to produce this reaction (for
example, by being too demanding), then she has more opportunity to change it.   Increasing self-awareness through giving
feedback is something which therapeutic communities are
ideally constructed to provide, both for staff and residents,
although staff often find it harder to give feedback to one
another than to residents.   An important point about acquir-
ing self-awareness is the part played by example or modelling.   When a staff member demonstrates her willingness to
learn something about herself, to say (when it's true) 'I
didn't realise I had that effect on you' or 'I realise I re-
acted that way because I was feeling unsupported', this can
provide a model for residents and other staff, taking hesi-
tant first steps towards learning about themselves.

Another kind of learning experience therapeutic community
staff ask for is 'the experience of being on the other side',
of being in the role of the patient, resident or client.
This indicates that,for all the emphasis on breaking down
barriers between staff and patient roles, there is still a
strong sense of 'them and us' which therapeutic community
staff have to understand and work with.   (This incidentally,
is no indictment of therapeutic communities for failing to
achieve their goal of greater equality between staff and
patients.   When familiar signs of difference are removed -
uniforms, titles, etc. - underlying barriers emerge more
starkly, without, as it were, the conventions that normally
clothe them.   For example, the convention of showing defer-
ence to those in authority may give way, when authority is
not exercised, to some more obvious form of avoiding personal
relationships.)

The experience of being in the patient's role is sought
for a number of reasons.   Staff feel it is a gap in their
experience, they are intrigued to know what it feels like.
Behind this may be some envy of those in the resident role,

both of their opportunities for personal learning and change,
and also their apparent freedom from the responsibilities and
constraints which the staff bear.   The urge to walk out of a
meeting, or just not turn up, to shout abuse at someone, or
worse, are not confined to residents.   The effort to contain
these impulses can be considerable, and may lead to resent-
ment, frustration, and disillusionment, heightened when
patients freely act them out.   In this situation the appeal
of reversing the roles is clear enough.

It may also be instructive, since the staff member-turned-
client will discover how it feels to be criticised by staff,
and pressured by his peers.   He will discover the pain as
well as the pleasure that follows from the greater license to
act on impulse.   And he will find out how the staff appear
from the patients' point of view.   Do they seem to be the
very same uncaring, critical, distant figures that residents
say he is?   The experience of being in the resident role can
have a profound effect on one's functioning as a staff
member.   Training in individual and group psychotherapy is
usually considered incomplete without the experiencing of
being in the patient role, and it is clearly felt by many
therapeutic community staff that their own training requires
a similar experience.

Another experience that therapeutic community staff seek
is 'being able to meet and talk with people who work in other
communities'.   The importance of this is often overlooked in
training courses, perhaps because it lies outside the 'cur-
riculum' of planned activities.   Yet half the people who
wanted to come on the training weekends gave this as one of
their three main reasons for applying.   For some this may
reflect the feeling of isolation in their own work, for
others it may mean a wish to get to know colleagues 'out of
role', to develop social relationships that complement working ones.   This is both pleasurable in itself - since we
surely have much in common with people who choose the same
kind of work - and creates the sense of belonging to a network of like-minded, well-disposed people, a sort of extended
family in which to exchange experiences, ideas and information.

People who work in therapeutic communities express a
fairly wide range of training needs, and the above grouping
is one way of putting these needs into some order.   The five
main needs which we have described are: knowledge about
therapeutic communities (both general and in terms of staff
roles), greater skill and effectiveness in therapeutic work,

personal awareness, experience of the residents' position,
and establishing contacts with colleagues in other communities.   Although this is a 'consumer' list, we think it
serves well as a basic framework.   We have sketched some of
the aspects which might arise under each heading, but have
not attempted to make a complete or systematic 'syllabus'.
That is a task to be pursued elsewhere.   Let us now turn
from needs to resources.

WHAT ARE THE RESOURCES FOR TRAINING AND LEARNING?

In the absence of a generally recognised training for therapeutic community work, each staff member has some scope to
decide for themselves what sorts of training to pursue and
what learning experiences best meet their own needs.   Why
training and learning?   We tend to use these words inter-
changeably, but it may be worth pausing to consider their
different implications.   When we speak of training we think
of experts, a prescribed series of steps, yardsticks of success, and a finished product: the trained person.   By contrast learning has a more personal meaning.   We can learn
from experts, but also from our peers, from those we try to
help, and in fact from any new experience that we enter with
an inquiring mind and our wits about us.   What we learn will
differ for each of us according to the sense we make of our
experience.

   Both training and learning are important in a therapeutic
community: training leads towards consistency of approach
and conformity to certain standards of behaviour, learning
leads towards individual autonomy and understanding.   In
practice, of course, we can 'learn' from a training course,
and may get 'trained' in the process of learning.   But the
distinction is worth bearing in mind.   In this section we
indicate a number of potential resources for learning and
training.   In the Information Section that follows we include a number of training courses and organisations.

Working in a therapeutic community

Earlier we discussed reasons why this may not provide sufficient opportunities for learning by itself, but no training
would make sense without it.   The experience cannot be
duplicated by books and lectures.   How much learning does
take place will depend among other things, on the community's
provision for supporting and training its new staff, on the

staff member's own willingness to learn, and on the general
level of morale and liveliness in the community at any particular time.

Given adequate morale in the community and openness in the
new member certain kinds of learning are almost bound to
occur.   Stereotypes about mental illness and deviance will
be broken down through participation with residents in everyday activities like washing up and gardening, and getting to
know people as individuals rather than as types or diagnoses.
The new member will learn some of the roles and techniques of
the staff (although not necessarily understanding them), and
will learn something about his or her own capacity for self-
reliance, assertiveness, and tolerance of uncertainty.

Learning about oneself, especially about what are felt as
one's inadequacies, may or may not be a constructive experience.   A lot depends on what sort of support is available.
Support may be provided in the regular staff feedback meetings, in a staff 'sensitivity' group, and through informal
staff relationships.   These are unlikely always to be enough
and there is a risk that the newcomer's anxieites and frustrations will not be adequately explored if these are the
only provisions available for doing so.   Someone working in
a therapeutic community for a month or so may not suffer too
much from this - may find it stimulating, revealing, and not
too upsetting to their own stability.   After leaving the
community they can continue to digest and think about the
experience.   For those who stay longer, the experience may
be too unsettling to learn from without additional sources of
supervision and training.

Supervision

Supervision can take place either within the therapeutic community or outside it.   Within the community one of the most
useful aspects of supervision is the regular time and space
it creates, set apart from the daily pressures and demands,
to think about events and one's own part in them.   The presence of the supervisor gives permission for such a period of
detachment and reflection, which may otherwise be difficult
to maintain in the middle of frequent requests for advice,
information, help, etc.

A distinction should be made between two meanings which
the term supervision can have in a therapeutic community.
One refers to the situation in which someone is responsible

for the work of a unit, or of a trainee, and oversees the
work being done, giving advice, correcting mistakes, and so
on.   This kind of supervision has a place in the administrative aspects of therapeutic communities - writing reports,
handling accounts, dealing with referrals.   Within the
sphere of psychotherapeutic activity supervision has a different meaning.   The supervisor helps the therapist to
understand the relationships between events in the community,
or in a particular group, taking into account the experience,
feelings, attitudes, etc. of all the participants.   Often
particular attention is given to the therapist's own responses.   The supervisor leaves the responsibility for deciding
how to respond to future events with the therapists.   This
contrasts with the former approach in which advice on the
best procedure is given.   In practice the two forms of
supervision may overlap a little but they are in principle
doing different things.   When people come together for
supervision it may be important to clarify expectation about
which sort of supervision is going to occur.

Various arrangements can be made for supervision.   Two
aspects which attract some debate are whether individual or
group supervision is better, and whether it is better for the
supervisor to be an experienced member of staff or an outside 'consultant'.   We do not think any procedure is necessarily to be preferred, and a lot will depend on who is
available, on the aims of the supervision and on the style of
the particular community.   New staff members often feel most
comfortable with regular individual sessions with a senior
staff member, and in many student 'placements' this is how
supervision is carried out.   This format offers the opportunity for in-depth discussion of the supervisee's personal
viewpoint and concerns, but this can often be enhanced in a
small group of three or four staff or trainees at a similar
stage in their work experience.   In addition to dealing with
the needs of particular staff members supervision may also be
concerned with certain activities such as group therapy, community meetings, or the functioning of the community as a
whole.   In these situations supervision will need to include
all the relevant staff members.

The position of the supervisor in relation to the rest of
the community has important implications.   Ideally he or she
should have a good understanding of the way the community
operates, but be sufficiently uninvolved in day-to-day events
to be able to stand back and take an overview.   An outside
consultant has the advantage of bringing a fresh viewpoint to
the community, but can also have disadvantages.   He may be

unaware of certain background issues affecting the staff, or
be unable to judge the impact of his own contribution after
he leaves.   On the other hand a staff member who is more in
touch with underlying issues and able to judge the effects of
his supervision, may be blinkered by his commitment to seeing
the community in a particular way.   Where a supervisor is
the director of the community or a senior staff member, difficulties may also arise from being seen as an authority
figure within the community.   How far this interferes with
supervision will depend on various factors, one important one
being whether the staff are also accountable to the supervisor for their work.   Wherever possible it is better if
supervision is not provided solely by the immediate superior
in a professional hierarchy.

   Outside the community supervision can be arranged on a
mutual, self-help basis.   Staff from two or more therapeutic
communities may form a group that meets regularly, taking it
in turns to present an issue or problem that has occurred in
one of their communities.   In such a group the topics often
concern recurring difficulties rather than immediate crises -
e.g. problems over staff leadership, attitudes towards sexual
relationships between residents, reactions to violence or
suicide.   Both the writers have participated in such a group
and found it valuable.   People who work in therapeutic communities understand each other's concerns very well.   They
can offer friendly, insightful, critical but constructive
observations, in a relatively threat-free atmosphere, since
turn by turn everyone is the learner and the supervisor.
Given two or more communities within travelling distance of
each other, the willingness to arrange periodic meetings and
roughly equivalent levels of work experience, such a group
has much to recommend it.   In addition to being able to discuss one's own community, there is also a unique opportunity
to learn how other communities function, in the kind of
detail that would otherwise require one to work there oneself.

Visiting other communities

It doesn't really matter what another community is like -
whether you agree with what they do, think they are better or
worse than you are - seeing and hearing about another therapeutic community is useful.   It raises questions, prompts
new ideas, and provides the stimulus to think about the way
you do things.   Even if they work with a different type of
resident or in a different setting, you will understand more
about your own community from seeing how another works, and

you may be able to establish useful links which can be developed for mutual learning and support.   When visiting established, well-known communities it is worth bearing in mind
that the image of a 'super-community' which has overcome all
the problems you are struggling with will probably turn out
to have been a mirage.   When you get close they are up
against the same tensions, cliques, defensiveness, and dis-
satisfactions as you thought you had left behind.   Finding
this out may reassure you that you are doing about as well as
anyone else, and perhaps better than you thought.

Reading

Reading is not a popular pastime in therapeutic communities.
The work itself is often exhausting, and reading about it may
seem like an additional burden.   Yet reading something which
helps you stand back from, and understand better, what it is
you are involved in with a particular resident or situation,
can actually help to make the work more bearable and interesting.   As an aid to reading you can arrange informal 'study
groups', where several people meet regularly to discuss
articles or books they have read, or which one person has
prepared comments on.   The to and fro between a paper and
the current life of your community is seldom dull.

Conferences, workshops, etc.

Conferences and other meetings - lectures, workshops, sym-
posia, seminars - come in all sizes and degrees of formality.
Seminars and workshops are typically fairly small (10-30
people) and allow opportunities for discussion or active participation.   Training workshops, taking place over a few
days, are an invaluable introduction to the experiential
aspect - the doing and the feeling - of working as a therapist.   Conferences are typically for a large number of
people, lasting anything from one day to a week.   They often
include social and fringe events that add to the interest of
the more formal parts and are a good way to meet people with
similar interests.

    In Britain the Association of Therapeutic Communities
arranges three one-day conferences each year and occasional
longer ones.   The recently formed World Federation of Therapeutic Communities holds an annual conference in a different
country each year.   In addition there are associations which
hold conferences and workshops for members of different pro-

fessional groups, and for those interested in particular
therapeutic techniques.   A number of these associations are
listed in the Information Section.

Experiential courses

An experiential course is one in which what you learn comes
from the actual experience of taking part in the course,
rather than from the information or opinions presented to you
by speakers.   The structure of an experiential course is
different from a conference or lecture, although some courses
combine the two kinds of learning.   An experiential course
is never fully structured, in the sense that a lecture is
fully structured - i.e. everyone knows exactly what they are
supposed to do throughout a lecture.   The time and the place
are set, there may be certain guidelines and there will be
one or more persons taking a training role of some kind.
But the actual events that take place are left to the spontaneous actions of the participants.   Faced with this situation people can and do react in a variety of ways: they may
stay silent, try to find out what the 'trainer' wants, com-
pete for leadership, agree to stick to safe topics, look for
partners, and so on.

What is the point of this kind of experience?   It helps
you learn about yourself, what sort of person you are, how
you deal with people and situations when the rules don't tell
you what to do.   It enables you to see different therapeutic
approaches and techniques as they happen, and more important-
ly, experience them from the patient's point of view.
You may also be able to practise taking the role of helper/
therapist/leader if you want to.   Some experiential courses
are set up to demonstrate a particular therapeutic approach -
e.g. psychodrama, group analysis, family therapy.   Others
offer a wider experience - e.g. therapeutic community living,
working in groups.   Some focus on a particular theme, such
as resistance in therapy, authority and leadership, cultural
differences.   Some have as their aim simply the sharing of
experience with others engaged in a similar work.

Whatever the stated aims or title, individuals attending
an experiential course are likely to have different experiences and learn different things, so perhaps the stated aims
should not be taken too much at face value.   Much will
depend on the personal styles of the staff running the
course, and the expectations and readiness to learn of the
individual participants.   If you are lucky, the content and

style of a course will fit with what you are ready to learn
about yourself as a person and as a therapist, but it is hard
to predict this in advance.

Experiential courses usually come in one of two lengths:
short, concentrated experiences which take place over a few
consecutive days, and groups which meet once a week for a
number of months.   Short courses can create an intense emotional experience, in which people are by turns extremely
anxious, happy, miserable, excited, and in which feelings of
great warmth, intimacy and closeness can occur, as well as
anger and distance.   Some people find this overwhelming,
others than it is of great benefit, others that it leaves
them relatively untouched.   One problem is that it is difficult to predict what your own experience will be, for the
reasons mentioned above, and once the emotions have subsided
there may be little long-term effect.

In following up people who attended one of the therapeutic
community training weekends mentioned earlier we found that a
year later about half the participants responded to a questionnaire and were able to recall details of the event.
Many of these reported small but significant changes in themselves, and a few had introduced some innovation into their
work as a result of the course.   The value of a short experiential course may, however, be as much in the break it provides, the opportunity for a shared experience which re-
freshes and reawakens interest and enthusiasm, as in the
longer-term effects 'back home'. (2)

Longer-term experiential courses allow time for the learning, and the putting into practice of what is learnt, to go
at a slower pace.   The experience is nearer to that of being
a patient in therapy - in fact the line between them may be
hard to draw except for the time available and the expectations of those involved.   A weekly experiential group may
lack the heady intensity of a short, residential course, but
allow for a more thorough and detailed exploration of individuals' experiences.   It also provides more opportunity to
experience and examine negative or ambivalent feelings.
These are often overlooked or not fully acknowledged in short
courses, which generate great cohesiveness and fellow feeling
between participants.

Participating in an experiential group, whether short or
long, provides an opportunity to share personal feelings and
attitudes in a relatively accepting atmosphere.   This effect
is probably greatest when the members do not work together or

have regular contact outside the group.   When they do,
issues of loyalty, confidentiality or accountability may
increase resistances to free discussion.   Such resistances
are inevitable in groups consisting of the staff in one particular community, who may have relationships both in and out
of work.   However, the first task of such groups is usually
to facilitate the work of the community rather than to provide the maximum opportunity for personal disclosure, and
they cannot be regarded as the equivalent of belonging to a
separate experiential group.

One further form of experiential learning of special value
in therapeutic community work is to join a therapeutic community as a resident for a time.   In this way you live, work
and feel alongside ordinary residents, without the distinction of being a student or the sense of it being a role play.
This approach to training operates in some concept-based
therapeutic communities for ex-addicts and in some psychotherapy training programmes such as those run by the Arbours
Association and Philadelphia Association, but is not generally available in hospital-based therapeutic communities.   A
simulated experience of being a resident in a therapeutic
community is also possible - as referred to earlier.

Personal therapy and training in psychotherapy

There are several reasons why personal therapy can be of
value.   Some of these have already been mentioned.   The
impact of working in a therapeutic community may reawaken
feelings of personal anxiety or unhappiness which need to be
explored;   and our interactions with patients or residents
will be more sensitive and empathic if we have experienced
for ourselves the pains and pleasures involved in personal
therapy.   Whatever the professional motives for seeking
therapy, it will only be of real value if there is a commitment to it for personal reasons.   While any training requires some personal motivation, seeking therapy can only be
a personal decision.   Participating in experiential courses
can give you some idea of what it will be like, to help you
decide if it is what you want.   If you do decide that you
want to have therapy, what are the options?

There are three considerations to bear in mind.   The
first is that you may have to pay for psychotherapy.   Psychotherapists who work privately charge fees which may be
high for students and low-paid staff, although some charge
lower fees for people on lower incomes.   If your organisa-

tion employs psychotherapists you may be able to obtain psychotherapy without payment.   Psychotherapists usually offer an initial session to discuss what you are looking for, and some offer a trial number of sessions.

A second consideration is whether to choose individual or group psychotherapy, and how frequent the sessions should be. Individual psychotherapy usually takes place once or twice a week but can be more frequent.   Group therapy is usually weekly, sometimes twice weekly.   If you are working in a therapeutic community and want to be able to relate your therapy to your work, group therapy may be more relevant. You will be able to appreciate directly the forces at work in a therapeutic group, and the presence of other patients in the group can help to break through the 'professional' way of thinking about problems that many mental health workers have. However, the choice of individual or group therapy is again a personal one, as well as being dependent on what is available, and both can be equally valuable.   In either case you should think in terms of 18 months upwards, although individual psychotherapy focused on a particular problem can be shorter than this.

A third consideration is the possibility of training as an individual or group psychotherapist.   Training usually takes from 2-5 years and includes personal psychotherapy (individual or group depending on the training), supervised work with patients and theoretical work.   If you are a student or newcomer this will probably be too great an undertaking to contemplate at the moment, but should you decide to stay in psychotherapeutic work then a full training at a recognised institute or centre may be worth considering.

MATCHING NEEDS AND RESOURCES

We have looked at the needs that therapeutic community staff describe, and at the resources which are potentially available to meet those needs.   If we place them side by side we can see which resources meet which needs.   Using this, together with the Information Section, may help you start to plan your own programme of training and learning.

Needs	Resources
Learning about the relevant theories, ideas and concepts and being able to apply them to your own work.	Books and articles by leading pioneers of therapeutic communities.

	Topical articles in journals.
	Attending conferences and courses in the fields of therapeutic communities, group psychotherapy, personal growth, psychoanalysis.
	Visiting other therapeutic communities.
	Supervision by someone with therapeutic community experience and/or training in psychotherapy, preferably group.
Practical training in relevant skills, techniques and roles. This includes being able to recognise processes going on in individuals, in a group and in the community as a whole.	Working in a therapeutic community, alongside more experienced staff.
	Regular supervision and/or mutual supervision between members of different groups or communities.
	Experiential courses and workshops.
Becoming more aware of yourself and how you relate to other people.	Working in a therapeutic community.
	Regular supervision and/or mutual supervision.
	Being a member of an experiential group meeting regularly, either ongoing with changing membership or time-limited (e.g. 6-12 months) with fixed membership.
	Personal group or individual psychotherapy.
The experience of being in the 'patient' or 'resident' role in a therapeutic community.	Being a member of an experiential/therapeutic group.
	Participating in a 'simulated therapeutic community.
	Spending some time as a resident in a therapeutic community.

Mutual exchange and support with other therapeutic community staff.	Mutual supervision/support group with members of other communities.
	Visiting other therapeutic communities, participating in conferences, workshops etc. - especially residential ones.
	Joining associations catering for staff with similar needs and interests.

As you can see, there is a good deal of overlap, with some resources meeting more than one need.   The order in which resources are listed is not meant to indicate any order of preference.   In practice, the more resources you can utilise the better, as they will tend to enhance each other. For example, working in a therapeutic community simultaneously combined with supervision, a mutual supervision group with other staff, participating in an experiential group and occasional conferences and workshops, will create opportunities for learning in one situation to be tried out in the others, which would not happen if you did one at a time.

You may be able to arrange some things yourself - e.g. a seminar group for discussing books and articles, visits to other communities, meeting with staff from other communities. Other resources such as supervision or experiential groups, tend to be more readily available in the larger cities where most psychotherapeutic work is carried out.   However, it is worth contacting training institutes and associations since they may have members in your area.   The Information section which follows will help you to locate resources available in the British regions and other countries.

Information on therapeutic communities, relevant associations and training opportunities

(written in collaboration with Jeff Roberts)

Our aim in this section is to give information which will help you to pursue your interest in therapeutic communities. We have included information from as many countries as possible and hope that most readers will find something of interest to them in their own country. The information has been collected by writing to people either known to us personally or through the Association of Therapeutic Communities. Although we have tried to spread our net as widely as possible, the result must inevitably be rather patchy and idiosyncratic. It should not be taken as fully representative of therapeutic communities in each country but as providing some initial points of contact.

Information of this kind is subject to change and it may be wise to preface inquiries by checking if the names and addresses given are still correct, especially if you are using this some years after 1982 when the information was collected.

Since both of us live and work in England we have been able to gather more information about resources in Great Britain than elsewhere, and this is presented first. Other countries are then presented in alphabetical order. Information for each country, where available, is presented under the following headings.

1 One or two well-established therapeutic communities. (They are usually able to receive interested visitors, but do not arrive without prior notice. Many communities have particular days for visitors.)

2 Associations which serve the interests of people working in therapeutic communities.

3 Training opportunities and the centres which provide
them.   (Some training opportunities may be restricted to
those who work in particular professions or work settings.)

4 Where the person providing the information has expressed willingness to be contacted by anyone wanting to find
out more this has been indicated.

We would like to express our gratitude to all those colleagues and contacts in Great Britain and abroad who answered
our queries and hope that in ordering and editing their information and comments we have not misrepresented what they told
us.

We would welcome comments, suggestions and corrections
with a view to updating for a future edition.   Please send
these to Jeff Roberts c/o the publishers.

GREAT BRITAIN

Therapeutic communities

In small specialised psychiatric hospitals

Cassel Hospital, 1 Ham Common, Richmond, Surrey TW10 7JF.
Henderson Hospital, 2 Homeland Drive, Sutton, Surrey SM2 5LT.
Ingrebourne Centre, St George's Hospital, Hornchurch, Essex.

In general psychiatric hospitals

Dingleton Hospital, Melrose, Roxburgh, Scotland.
Littlemore Hospital, Oxford (Phoenix Unit, Eric Burden
    Community).
Fulbourn Hospital, Cambridge (Street Ward, Burnet House).

In hostels for ex-psychiatric patients

Richmond Fellowship has numerous hostels and half-way houses
around Great Britain.   Headquarters address: 8 Addison Road,
London W14 8DL.

In schools for maladjusted children and adolescents

The Cotswold Community, Ashton Keyns, Nr Swindon,
    Wilts SN6 6QN.
New Barns School, Church Lane, Toddington, Gloucester.
Peper Harow, Godalming, Surrey GU8 6BG.

In day centres

St Luke's Project, Kensington and Chelsea Social Services
Dept, Old Town Hall, Kings Road, London SW3 5EE.

*In schools and communities for handicapped children and
adults*

There are numerous communities based on the ideas of Rudolf
Steiner.   For further information: The Camphill Village
Trust, Delrow House, Aldenham, Watford, Herts WD2 8DJ.

In a prison for young offenders

HM Prison Grendon, Grendon Underwood, Aylesbury,
    Bucks HP18 0TL.

For drug addicts ('concept-based')

Alpha House, Wickham Road, Droxford, Hants.
Ley Community, Sandy Croft, Sandy Lane, Yarnton, Oxon OX5 1PB.
Phoenix House, 1 Eliot Bank, London SE23.

As an alternative to psychiatric treatment

The Arbours Crisis Centre, 41 Weston Park, London N8.
Philadelphia Association, 74a Portland Road, London W11 4LQ.

Associations serving the interests of therapeutic community
workers

Association of Therapeutic Communities.   Membership inquir-
ies to Dr Stuart Whiteley, ATC Membership Secretary,
Henderson Hospital, 2 Homeland Drive, Sutton, Surrey SM2 5LT.
General inquiries to David Kennard, ATC Secretary, c/o
Rampton Hospital, Retford, Notts DN22 0PD.

European Federation of Therapeutic Communities (primarily concerned with drug addiction).   Inquiries to Dave Tomlinson, Chairman, European Federation of Therapeutic Communities (UK and Eire Section), Phoenix House, 1 Eliot Place, London SE23.

Planned Environment Therapy Trust (concerned with schools for maladjusted children).   Inquiries to John Cross, New Barns School, Church Lane, Toddington, Nr Cheltenham, Gloucs.

Association of Workers in Maladjusted Schools.   Inquiries to Rodney Smith, Glebe House, Shudy Camps, Cambridge.

Group Analytic Society.   1 Daleham Gardens, London NW3.

Association for Family Therapy.   Numerous local branches. Inquiries to Hugh Jenkins, 17 Powy's Drive, Dinas Powis, South Glamorgan CF6 4LN.

Organisations offering training courses and events related to therapeutic community work.

We are grateful to the following people for helping to provide us with the information and addresses included here: Pamela Ashurst, David Clark, Barbara Dick, Graeme Farquharson, John Harrington, Peter Hawkins, Keith Hyde, Hugh Koch, Terry Lear, Michael O'Reilly, Lesley Reid and Terry Veitch.

National and London area

Association of Therapeutic Communities

Training activities include: one year course, short residential courses, regular conferences, supervisors group, peer self-help groups.   (See Associations for address.)

Henderson Hospital

Group Work Course.   This one-term course is planned to include ideas relevant to therapeutic community work.   Inquiries to The Secretary, The Henderson Hospital, 2 Homeland Drive, Sutton, Surrey.

Institute of Group Analysis (see also regional courses)

Training activities include: introductory group work course,
advanced group work course, qualifying course (leading to
membership of the institute).   Workshops and seminars on
various themes.   Enquiries to the Administrator, Institute
of Group Analysis, 1 Daleham Gardens, London NW3.

Tavistock Institute of Human Relations

Conferences and other events giving special emphasis to
intergroup relations, authority and leadership.   Address:
Tavistock Institute of Human Relations, 120 Belsize Lane,
London NW3 5BA.

Arbours Association

Training in dynamic psychotherapy which includes a 6-month
placement in a therapeutic community.   Preliminary seminars
are available to associates.   Address: The Arbours Association, 41 Weston Park, London N8.

Richmond Fellowship

Two-year in-service training for hostel staff plus regular
short courses for therapeutic community workers.   Address:
Richmond Fellowship, 8 Addison Road, London W14.

South and south-west

Southampton

Wessex Psychotherapy Society holds regular monthly meetings.
People working in a therapeutic community would be welcomed
as members of this society.   Staff of the Royal South Hants
Hospital can take advantage of training opportunities in the
psychotherapy department.   Supervision seminars are available.   Information on these and related activities is available from The Psychotherapy Department, Department of Psychiatry, Royal South Hants Hospital, Graham Road, Southampton
SO9 4PE.

Counselling skills, Transactional Analysis, Action Techniques: courses and training weekends are offered by the
adult education department of the University of Southampton.

A course in counselling is offered by the Southampton
Pastoral Counselling Service, Union Road, Northam,
Southampton.

Bristol/Bath

Bristol Psychotherapy Association provides information on
local resources.   Write to Richard Tillet, Glenside Hospital,
Blackberry Hill, Stapleton, Bristol.

A two-year course in Facilitator Styles (humanistic psy-
chology approach) is sponsored jointly by the Centre for the
Study of Organisational Change and Development, and the
Institute for the Development of Human Potential.   Write to
Peter Reason, Centre for the Study of Organisational Change
and Development, University of Bath, Claverton Down, Bath.

Further information about training activities and resources for therapeutic community workers can be obtained through
Peter Hawkins, Centre for the Study of Organisational Change
and Development (address as above).

Devon

Holwell Centre for Psychodrama - offers residential training
weekends and weeks, and a diploma course in Psychodrama.
Inquiries to East Down, Barnstaple, North Devon EX31 4NZ.

Wales

Cardiff

Drama Therapy Workshops are run by the Institute of Family
Therapy.   Write to Roy Suttleworth, Institute of Family
Therapy, Cathedral Road, Cardiff.

There are two therapeutic community wards in Whitchurch
Hospital, so that in-service training is feasible in the area.
Write to Hugh Koch, Whitchurch Hospital, Cardiff.

Midlands

Oxford

One-year Midland Course in Group Work and Family Therapy in association with the Institute of Group Analysis in London. Write to Ann West, Littlemore Hospital, Oxford.

One-year Counselling Course - 'an interdisciplinary course for those helping others'. Write to The Youth and Community Training Officer, Education Dept, Oxfordshire County Council, Macclesfield House, Oxford OX1 1NA.

One-year (full-time) Course in Psychodynamic Nursing for selected psychiatric nurses. Write to JBCNS Course Tutor, Nurse Training School, Littlemore Hospital, Oxford OX4 4XN.

Psychotherapy Workshops and Training Groups are arranged by the Psychotherapy Department, Warneford Hospital, Oxford.

Northampton

One-year Midland Course in Group Work and Family Therapy in association with the Institute of Group Analysis in London. Write to Mrs Rose Fisher, Cheyne Walk Clinic, 3 Cheyne Walk, Northampton.

Birmingham

Two-year Introductory Psychotherapy Course in Individual and Group Psychotherapy, giving eligibility for membership of the West Midlands Institute of Psychotherapy. Write to The Centre for Post-Graduate Psychiatry, Uffculme Clinic, Queens-bridge Road, Moseley, Birmingham B13 8QD.

One-year (full-time) course in Psychodynamic Nursing, for selected psychiatric nurses. Address as above.

Supervision and participation in groups as co-therapists can be arranged for those who have already undergone basic training. Write to West Midlands Institute of Psychotherapy, c/o as above.

East Anglia

Cambridge

One-year General Course in Group Work, run in association
with the Institute of Group Analysis (London).   Write to Mrs
Julie Aston, Fulbourn Hospital, Cambridge CB1 5EF.

   In-service training is possible within the various therapeutic communities which continue to flourish at Fulbourn
Hospital.   Inquiries should be made by staff members in the
appropriate department at Fulbourn Hospital.

North-west

Manchester

One-year Introductory Group Work Course, in association with
the Institute of Group Analysis (London).   Write to Dr Keith
Hyde, Consultant Psychotherapist, Prestwich Hospital, Bury
New Road, Prestwich, Manchester.

   Annual workshops in psychotherapy are run by the regional
health authority.   Write to Regional Training Officer, North
West Regional Health Authority, Gateway House, Piccadilly
South, Manchester M60 7LP.

   A course in Family Therapy is run by the Institute of
Family Therapy.   Write to Dr M. Davenport, Consultant Child
Psychiatrist, Booth Hall Hospital, Charlestown Road,
Manchester 9.

Scotland

Edinburgh

A two-year course in Analytical Groups and an introductory
course in Family Therapy are run by the Scottish Institute of
Human Relations, 56 Albany Street, Edinburgh EH1 3QR.

   There are various courses on working with groups, leadership, understanding society and institutions.   Write to Mr J.
Callan Anderson, Secretary/Organising Tutor, South East Scotland Training Association, Moray House College of Education,
Holyrood Road, Edinburgh EH8 2AQ.

Courses on various aspects of psychotherapy and counselling, including Transactional Analysis and Gestalt Therapy, are run under the auspices of the Dept of Extra-Mural Studies, University of Edinburgh, Buccleuch Place, Edinburgh.

Melrose

An in-service training in Therapeutic Community Work and Community Psychiatry, particularly Crisis Intervention is offered to staff members at Dingleton Hospital, Melrose, Roxburghshire TD6 9HN.

Personal psychotherapy

Some experience of personal psychotherapy is an important part of training for those who intend to work in a therapeutic community for more than a brief time. (The reasons for this are discussed in Chapter 10.) Some training courses include such experience, but many do not.

It is possible to obtain either individual or group psychotherapy in most of the regions we have listed. In some cases the centres which provide training are also able to offer personal therapy. If you want further information about the availability of personal therapy in your area, you can do one or more of the following:

if you have any friends or colleagues who have had psychotherapy talk to them about it - they may be able to recommend someone;

if there is a consultant psychotherapist at a nearby psychiatric hospital, talk to him or her;

contact one of the local training centres listed here;

if you are unable to talk to people locally you can contact one of the psychotherapy organisations in London. They may be able to put you in touch with one of their members living in your area.

Below are the names and addresses of some of the larger organisations:

The London Clinic of Psychoanalysis (part of the Institute of Psychoanalysis), 63 New Cavendish Street, London W1M 7RD.

London Centre for Psychotherapy, 19 St Fitzjohn's Avenue,
Swiss Cottage, London NW3 5YJ.

British Association of Psychotherapists, 121 Hendon Lane,
London N3.

Society of Analytical Psychology, 1 Daleham Gardens,
London NW3.

The Institute of Group Analysis, 1 Daleham Gardens,
London NW3.

AUSTRALIA

Victoria

Professor A.W. Clark of La Trobe University writes:

Therapeutic communities of various sorts come and go in
Australia, often depending on the ability of administrative systems to tolerate physical disruption and violence.

A Victorian one that has survived for $3\frac{1}{2}$ years is Toad
Hall; it is situated in Royal Park Psychiatric Hospital,
Melbourne, and Dr Bill McLeod is the medical director.
In country hospitals in Victoria, Dr John Bomford heads a
unit in Bendigo and Dr Max Wellstead one in Beechworth.
These, like Toad Hall, have some but not all of the
defining characteristics of a 'classic' therapeutic com-
munity.

Western Australia

Dr A.J. Stubley sends the following information:

Therapeutic communities

Biala, Weir Road, Mundaring, Western Australia, 6053.
Richmond Fellowship of W.A., 13 Teague Street, Victoria
     Park, Western Australia, 6100.
Niola Private Hospital, 67 Cambridge Street, Leederville,
     Western Australia, 6007.
There are well-established therapeutic communities in
Perth.   The equivalent Richmond Fellowship community
exists in each state of Australia.   (See below.)

Training

No organised training offered.   Day-to-day informal training offered to staff at Niola Private Hospital.

Dr Stubley would be glad to act as a point of contact for people interested in therapeutic communities in Australia, and can be contacted either at 'Biala' or Niola Private Hospital.

New South Wales

There are a number of concept-based therapeutic communities for drug abusers in NSW, these include:

The Buttery, Lismore Road, Binna Burra, Bungalow, NSW 2479.

Killara House, 566 Wyse Street, Albury, NSW 2640.

Odyssey House, 24 Roslyn Street, Elizabeth Bay, NSW 2011.

The Richmond Fellowship has houses in Canberra, NSW, Queensland, Victoria and Western Australia.   For further information write to: The Richmond Fellowship of Australia, 196 Flinders Street, Melbourne 3000, Victoria.

AUSTRIA

We have no direct information, but the Richmond Fellowship has two houses, one in Vienna and one in Mistelbach.   For further information write to: The Richmond Fellowship of Oesterreich, Schmoellerlgasse 5/9, 1040 Vienna.   Tel.: 0222/65 70 262.

BELGIUM

Dr S. Verhaest, Universitair Psychiatrisch Centrum v.z.w., St Jozef, 3070 Kortenberg, Leuvensesteenweg 517, sends the following information.

Therapeutic communities

Universitair Psychiatrisch Centrum St Jozef, Leuvensesteenweg 517, B-3070 Kortenberg.   Psychotherapeutic communities for adults, for adolescents, day centre.

Psychotherapeutisch Centrum Rustenburg, Oude Oostende Steenweg 43, B-8000 Brugge.   Psychotherapeutic community for adults.

Associations

There is no specific Flemish Association, but there are strong links with the Dutch 'Vereniging voor Werkers in Psychotherapeutische Gemeenschappen'.

The 'Vlaamse Verenigning voor Groepsychotherapie' has many members working in residential group psychotherapy and holds meetings twice a year.   Address: Keizersvest 22, B-9000 Gent.

Training

The Postgraduate Course in Psychoanalytic Psychotherapy of the University of Leuven gives training to psychiatrists and psychologists, which includes training in residential group psychotherapy.   Address: Universitair Psychiatrisch Centrum St Jozef, Leuvensesteenweg 517, B-3070 Kortenberg.

Dr Verhaest is willing for interested people to contact him.

BRAZIL

Dr Jorge P. Ribeiro, of the Universidade de Brasilia, sends the following information.

Therapeutic communities

Communidade Terapeutica 'Crianca', Rua Coimbra, No. 5, 09900 Diadema, Sp. Brasil.   Director: Dr Oswaldo Di Loreto, Rua Professor Atilio Inocente, No. 603, 04538 S. Paulo, Sp. Brasil.

Clinica Sante Fe, 13.970 Itapira, Sao Paulo, Brasil. Director: Dr Helio Amancio de Camargo.

Hospital Pinel, 90.000 Porto Elegre, RS. Brasil. Director: Dr Marcelo Blays Peres.

GREECE

Therapeutic community

Open Psychotherapeutic Centre, 9-11 S Charalambi and Ch.
Trikoupi, str., Athens 708, Greece.   Director of Training
and Research: Dr Ioannis Tsegos, who is willing for interested people to contact him at the above address.

HOLLAND

There are many therapeutic communities in Dutch psychiatric
hospitals and day hospitals.

    Dr Lout van Eck, Provincial Ziekenhuis to Santpoort,
Postbus 50, Santpoort Zuid, Brederodelaan 54, sends the following information.

Therapeutic communities

De Oosthoek, Oosterzijweg 8, 1906 ZA Limmen (NH), refer to
Wout Kooiman.

    'Rijnland', Provinciaal Ziekenhis Santpoort, Brederode-
laan 54, 2080 AB Santpoort, refer to Peter Bierenbroodspot.

Association

Vereniging van Werkers in Psychotherapeutische Gemeenschappen
(VWPG), Secretary - Stefan van den Langenberg, c/o Provincial
Ziekenhuis, Santpoort (address as above).

    Dr Van Eck is willing for interested people to contact him.

ISRAEL

Professor Stanley Schneider, Director, Summit, Institute, 44
Shimoni Street, Jerusalem wirtes: 'Israel is just beginning
to develop in this area.   While group psychotherapy has been
an accepted modality, the use of therapeutic communities is
limited.'

Therapeutic communities

Summit Institute, Shimoni 44, Jerusalem, Israel.   A Network
of Psychiatric Treatment Services which treats male and
female adolescents and young adults within residential treatment centres, half-way houses, and transitional home apart-
ments.   Director: Professor Stanley Schneider.

N'nai Brith Children's Home and Group House, Bayit V'Gan,
Jerusalem, Israel (P.O.B. 16017).   A residential treatment
centre, and group half-way house.   Director: Yecheskiel
Cohen.

Training

Summit Institute provides training for work in therapeutic
communities and therapeutic milieus.

Dr Schneider would be happy to serve as a resource for
people visiting Israel seeking information on therapeutic
communities.

JAPAN

Professor Masaaki Kato, Director, National Institute of
Mental Health, sends the following information.

Therapeutic communities

Kaijo-ryo Sanatorium (Director: Junichi Suzuki), Nonaka 4017,
Asahi-she, Chiba-ken, Japan 289-25.

Takajaya Prefectural Hospital, Komori-machi 2225-1,
Takajaya, Tsu-shi, Mie-ken, Japan 514.

Association

Japan Society of Group Psychotherapy, c/o Dr Yamaguchi, Dept
of Psychiatry, Nihon Medical College, Sendagi 1-1-5, Bunkyo-
ku, Tokyo, Japan 113.

Dr Junichi Suzuki, Director, Maijo-ryo Sanatorium (see
above) can be contacted for further information.

NEW ZEALAND

We have no direct information, but the Richmond Fellowship of
New Zealand has three houses, in Auckland, Christchurch and
Wellington.   For further information write to Mrs Peggy
Ziesler, National Co-ordinator, The Richmond Fellowship of
New Zealand, 4 Pickett Avenue, Mt Albert, Auckland 3.

NORWAY

Dr Jarl Jørstad, Medical Director, Ulleval Sykehus 6B, Psychiatric Department, Oslo 1, writes: 'The whole area of therapeutic communities in Norway has been in a stage of change
because of the reorganisation and sectorisation of our whole
psychiatric care system.'

Therapeutic communities

'This department has for 20 years been the pioneer unit where
the therapeutic community started in Norway, and where the
model was practised and more or less spread to other hospi-
tals/units.   Now our acute psychiatric unit has been re-
organised, and the therapeutic community is much modified.
Our day unit, situated in another building close to the
acute unit, is developing a more clear-cut therapeutic community for 15 to 20 patients.'

   Another well-established therapeutic community is Dikemark
Hospital, Department 5 (Lien), 1385 Solberg, situated 30 km
outside Oslo.

Association

The psychotherapy section of Norwegian Psychiatric Association serves the interest of all those who work individually,
with groups, and also in therapeutic communities.

Training

There is no special organisation which provides training of
particular relevance to therapeutic community staff.   This
is done in the different departments where the therapeutic
community is practised.

More detailed information about therapeutic communities
in Norway is available from Herluf Thomstad, M.D., Bergsal-
leen 13, Oslo 3, or from Dr Jørstad.

SWEDEN

Dr Goran Ahlin, Overlakore, Unit of Training in Psychotherapy,
Longbro Sjukhus, 125 85 Alvsjo, writes: 'On the whole the
emphasis on development towards therapeutic community has had
a peak in the beginning of the 1970s and is now more weak in
general.   A number of institutions have been closed down by
their administration and/or the surrounding structure.   At
the same time traditional care, both in the psychiatric and
in the social fields, claim to have "incorporated" ideas from
therapeutic community movements.   This is, in my opinion,
wrong and more an expression of so-called repressive tolerance.'

Therapeutic communities

'One of the oldest therapeutic community units which still
functions very well is the Day Hospital of Fruangen
(Fruangens Dagsjukhus) situated in one of the southern sub-
urbs of Stockholm, close to the Mental Hospital of Langbro
(Langbro Sjukhus) to which it is linked administratively.
The address is Fruangens kyrkogata 14, 126 65 Hagersten.
There is one example of the whole clinic developing in therapeutic community direction, the clinic for general psychiatry
of Boden.   Its address is Psykiatriska kliniken, Centrallas-
arettet, 961 19 Boden.   One of the best-known therapeutic
community units in the social care field is the Vallmotorp,
an institution for adult alcoholics.   The address is
Stiftelsen Vallmotorp, 641 00 Katrineholm.   It is situated
close to a small town south-west of Stockholm.'

Association

'An association aimed at support for staff of therapeutic
communities was formed in 1980 at a meeting at the Vallmotorp
mentioned above.   It mainly has members from the social care
and less from the psychiatric side.   This "association for
milieu therapy" can be reached through Lars Bremberg, head of
the Vallmotorp.'

Training

'The organisations coming closest to assist in training for staff of therapeutic communities nowadays are those offering training in psychotherapy both in the universities of Stockholm and Umea and the similar trainings in psychotherapy in different parts of the country.'

Dr Ahlin adds: 'Although I have left the active involvement in therapeutic communities for my present work as a consultant and trainer in psychotherapy - at Langbro Hospital - I may still be one of those who have information about the development of therapeutic community movement in the country.'

SWITZERLAND

Professor Edgar Heim, Psychiatrische Universitatspoliklinik Bern, 3010 Bern, Murtenstrasse 21, sends the following information.

Therapeutic communities

Psychiatrische Klinik Schlossli, 8618 Oetwil a.S. / ZH : 400 bed teaching hospital serving a catchment area.   'Since 1968 a therapeutic community has been systematically established and is spread on all wards.   The concept is still well preserved in spite of a change of leadership in 1978.

Beside this systematic therapeutic community there are now several hospitals aiming in the same direction:

Psychiatrische Klinik, 4410 Liestal /BL.

Psychiatrische Universitatspoliklinik, 3010 Bern.

'There also exists a large number of the "new kind" (concept-based) of therapeutic communities dealing with drug patients.   Information could be provided by Professor Ambros Uchtenhagen, Direktor des Sozial-psychiatrischen Dienstes der Psychiatrischen Universitatsklinik, Langgstrasse 31, 8029 Zurich 8.'

Professor Heim adds: 'Besides therapeutic communities including an entire hospital as mentioned above, there are quite a number of psychotherapeutic communities on a ward level.   I would be glad to give anyone interested in it more accurate information.'

UNITED STATES

The United States is the home of concept-based therapeutic communities for ex-drug addicts, and therapeutic communities of this type are numerically the greatest in the USA.   We give information about these first.

   Dr George De Leon, Director of Research and Evaluation, Phoenix House Foundation, New York, sends the following information.

Therapeutic communities

Two well-established therapeutic communities are:

   Phoenix House Foundation, 164 West 74th Street, New York, NY 10023.

   Daytop Village, 54 West 40th Street, New York, NY 10019.

Association

Therapeutic Communities of America is a national organisation of therapeutic communities.   Write to TCA, c/o Gateway Houses Foundation, 624 South Michigan Avenue, Chicago, Illinois 60605, USA.

Training

Phoenix House Foundation provides training of particular relevance to therapeutic community staff.

   The National Institute on Drug Abuse (NIDA), a branch of the US Dept of Health and Human Services, is an agency that is able to provide a broad range of information concerning drug and alcohol use/abuse, e.g. treatments, research, evaluation, etc.

Other types of therapeutic community:

Therapeutic communities

Soteria House, c/o Mental Health Research Institute, 555 Middlefield Road, Palo Alto, California.

Spring Lake Ranch, Rutland, Vermont (a rural community for the chronic mentally ill, student helpers and long-term staff).

The Richmond Fellowship has eleven houses in the United States along the Eastern seaboard.   For further information write to: The Richmond Fellowship of America, 25 Riverside Drive, New York, NY 10023.

Training

Professor Rudolf Moos writes from Stanford University Medical Center, California: 'In regard to training, some of the experiences offered by the Esalen Institute in Big Sur are certainly relevant.   In general, however, the relevant training either occurs in particular seminars in masters or doctoral level programs in social work, psychology, and so forth, or occurs "on the job" as an intern or trainee in one of the communities themselves.'

WEST GERMANY

Professor Andreas Ploeger, Abteilung Medizinische Psychologie, Hans-Bocker-Allee, 5100 Aachen, West Germany, sends the following information.

Therapeutic communities

(a) In the sector of psychiatry: Psychiatrisches Landeskrankenhaus, Hermann-Simon Strasse, D14830 Gutersloh.

Psychiatrisches Landeskrankenhaus, Hermann Pesche Strasse, 4070 Rheydt/Monchengladbach.

(b) In the sector of psychotherapy: Haus fur Neurosekranke, Christian Belser Strasse, 7000 Stuttgart-Sonnenberg.

Association

Deutsche Gesellschaft fur soziale Psychiatrie in der
Bundesrepublik Deutschland e.V., Wrede Strasse 2, 3000
Hannover.

Training

Psychiatrische Universitatsklinik der Medizinischen Hoch-
schule, D-3000 Hannover-Kleefeld.

Professor Ploeger adds: 'If somebody wants to find out
more about therapeutic communities in Germany, they could
contact me.   I have contacts in nearly all colleges working
in this area in Western Germany (Federal Republik of Germany)
and also in the eastern part of our country (German Demokratic
Republik).'

YUGOSLAVIA

Dr Milos Kobal, Professor of Psychiatry at Klinicni Center v
Ljubljani, sends the following information.

Therapeutic communities

Institut za mentalno zdravlje, Palmoticeva 37, 11000 Beograd.

Psihijatrijska klinika, Klinicki bolnicki centar Rebro,
Kispaticeva 12, 41000 Zagreb.

Klinika za neurologiju, psihijatriju i alcoholisam i druge
ovisnosti, Klinicka bolnica 'Dr Mladen Stojanovic',
Vinogradska, 41000 Zagreb.

Center za mentalno zdravje, Poljanski nasip 58,
61000 Ljubljana.

Training

In the postgraduate courses on psychotherapy at University
Medical Schools in Beograd, Zagreb, and Ljubljana, a training
for therapeutic communities is also provided.   Themes dealing with therapeutic communities are often dealt with in the
School of Institutional Psychiatry at Petrinja/Sisak/.

Further information on concept-based therapeutic communities in Europe and elsewhere may be obtained from:

European Federation of Therapeutic Communities, Dok Zuid 25, 9000 Gent, Belgium.

World Federation of Therapeutic Communities, 54 West 40th Street, New York, NY 10018, USA.

Recommended reading

BASIC PSYCHOTHERAPEUTIC IDEAS

What is Psychotherapy?, Jerome Frank, in 'An Introduction to
the Psychotherapies', Sidney Bloch (ed.), Oxford Univer-
sity Press, 1979.
'Introduction to Psychotherapy - An Outline of Psychodynamic
Principles and Practices', Dennis Brown and Jonathan
Pedder, London: Social Science Paperbacks (1979) (espec-
ially Part 2).
'The Art of Psychotherapy', Anthony Storr, London: Secker &
Warburg/Heinemann, 1979.
'On Becoming a Person: A therapist's view of psychotherapy,
Carl Rogers, Boston: Houghton-Mifflin, 1951.

INTRODUCTIONS TO GROUP PSYCHOTHERAPY

'Group Approaches in Psychiatry', J. Stuart Whiteley and
John Gordon, London: Routledge & Kegan Paul, 1979.
'The Theory and Practice of Group Psychotherapy', Irwin D.
Yalom, New York: Basic Books, 1975.
'Small Group Psychotherapy', Henry Walton (ed.), Harmonds-
worth: Penguin Books, 1971.
'Group Psychotherapy', S.H. Foulkes and E.J. Anthony, Har-
mondsworth: Penguin, 1965.

THERAPEUTIC COMMUNITIES IN PSYCHIATRIC SETTINGS

'Social Therapy in Psychiatry' (2nd edn), David Clark, Edin-
burgh: Churchill Livingstone, 1981.
'Social Psychiatry in Practice', Maxwell Jones, Harmondsworth,
Penguin, 1968.

'Community as Doctor', Robert Rapoport, London: Tavistock,
    1960.
'The Large Group', Lionel Kreeger (ed.), London: Constable,
    1975.   (Introduction and Chapters 1, 2, 6, 7 are rele-
    vant.)

THERAPEUTIC COMMUNITIES IN NON-HOSPITAL SETTINGS

'The Therapeutic Community Outside the Hospital', Elly Jansen
    (ed.), London: Croom Helm, 1980.   (Based on the work of
    the Richmond Fellowship.)
'I Haven't Had to go Mad Here', Joe Berke, Harmondsworth:
    Penguin, 1979.   (The anti-psychiatry approach.)
'Daytop Village - A Therapeutic Community', by Barry Sugarman,
    New York: Holt, Rinehart & Winston, 1974.   (Ex-addict
    self-help community.)
'Spare the Child - The Story of an Experimental Approved
    School', David Wills, Harmondsworth: Penguin Education
    Special, 1971.

RECENT DEVELOPMENTS AND RESEARCH

'Therapeutic Communities - Reflections and Progress',
    Hinshelwood and Manning (eds), London: Routledge & Kegan
    Paul, 1979.
The usefulness of groups in clinical settings, Peter B. Smith,
    Heather Wood and Gerald G. Smale, in 'Small Groups and
    Personal Change', (ed.) Peter B. Smith, London: Methuen,
    1980.
Recent British work on the therapeutic community, David
    Millard, in 'Current Themes in Psychiatry', vol. 3 (eds),
    R.N. Gaind, I.F. Fawzy, R.O. Pasnau, New York: Spectrum,
    1982.

STAFF TRAINING AND RELATED ISSUES

On being a good enough staff member, Monica Meinrath and
    Jeff Roberts, in 'International Journal of Therapeutic
    Communities', vol. 3, no. 1, 1982, pp. 7-14.
'Burn Out - Stages in the Disillusionment of the Helping Pro-
    fession', Jerry Edelwich and Archie Brodsky, New York:
    Human Sciences Press, 1980.
The Ailment, Tom Main, in 'British Journal of Medical Psychol-
    ogy', 30, pp. 129-45, 1957.   Reprinted in 'Psychosocial
    Nursing', Elisabeth Barnes (ed.), London: Tavistock Press,
    1968.

INTRODUCTION TO OTHER THERAPIES USED IN THERAPEUTIC
COMMUNITIES

'Acting-in: Practical Applications of Psychodramatic Methods',
    Howard Blatner, New York: Springer, 1973.
'Creative Therapy', Sue Jennings, London: Pitman, 1975.
'On Not Being Able to Paint', Marian Milner, London: Heine-
    mann, 1971.

REGULAR PUBLICATION

'International Journal of Therapeutic Communities', published
    by the Association of Therapeutic Communities (see under
    Great Britain - Associations).

Notes

1 DIFFERENT ORIGINS - COMMON ATTRIBUTES

1 Readers interested in reading more about traditional
   institutions are recommended to read Erving Goffman's
   classic 'Asylums' (1961), a compelling if one-sided
   account of the 'total institution'. The term 'therapeutic community approach' was introduced by David Clark
   (1965), who has also written more recently on international developments in the use of therapeutic community
   ideas (Clark, 1977).
2 Clark (1965).
3 Bessin (1977). Since Chapter 1 was written, in 1980,
   there have been increasing signs that therapeutic communities derived from Synanon do recognise the existence,
   and importance, of the 'democratic' type of therapeutic
   community developed by Maxwell Jones.
4 Clark (1977).
5 Rapoport (1960).
6 Clark (1965).
7 Main (1946).
8 For a discussion of the importance of therapeutic
   rationales for combating demoralisation see Frank (1979).
9 Hobson (1979) offers a serious but entertaining discussion of the problems of the messianic community. The
   closure in the late 1970s of two long-established therapeutic community day hospitals has given rise to much
   soul-searching discussion. See, for example, 'International Journal of Therapeutic Communities', vol. 1, no.
   3, which is devoted to papers dealing with destructive
   processes in therapeutic communities. This issue is
   also discussed in this book in relation to Synanon - see
   Chapter 5.

2   THE INSTITUTIONAL THERAPEUTIC COMMUNITY

1   My account of the development of moral treatment in the
    United States is based on David Rothman's extremely read-
    able history, 'The Discovery of the Asylum' (1971).
2   Scull (1979), p. 142.
3   More is said about Laing's ideas in the chapter on anti-
    psychiatry.   The role of the established professions is
    challenged by Illich et al. (1977).
4   Scull (1979).
5   I am indebted to Susan Michie for providing me with a
    copy of a report published by the Havana Psychiatric Hos-
    pital in 1971.
6   I am grateful to Dr Bertram Mandelbrote for providing me
    with background information on this period of development
    in British psychiatry.   Many of these developments were
    brought together in 'Psychiatric Hospital Care' edited by
    Freeman (1965).   Several of the pioneers of institution-
    al therapeutic communities produced exciting, optimistic
    books about their efforts and ideas.   See, for example,
    Clark (1964), Martin (1962), Schoenberg (1972).
7   Maller (1971).   The question of how to change staff
    roles in an institution has also been discussed recently
    by a Swedish psychiatrist, Goran Ahlin (1981).
8   The atmospheres of wards in different psychiatric hospi-
    tals have been measured with the Ward Atmosphere Scale
    developed by Rudolf Moos (1974).   He found that thera-
    peutic community wards have a distinctive atmosphere when
    contrasted with other types of ward.   They were charac-
    terised by relatively high levels of involvement, spon-
    taneity, concern with personal problems and tolerance of
    anger and aggression, and with a low level of staff con-
    trol (Price and Moos, 1975) .

3   DEMOCRACY AND PSYCHOANALYSIS

1   In fact these concepts can be more complex than is sug-
    gested here.   Countertransference may also include the
    second person's own transference.   For further discus-
    sion of these and other psychoanalytic concepts see Brown
    and Pedder (1979) and Storr (1979).
2   An excellent introduction to these processes, especially
    as they occur in large group meetings, is Tom Main's
    chapter, Some psychodynamics of large groups, in 'The
    Large Group' (Kreeger, 1975).
3   This account is drawn from 'Pioneer Work with Maladjusted
    Children', by Maurice Bridgeland (1971), which the inter-

ested reader is recommended to consult for detailed
accounts of the work of the pioneers referred to here.
I am also indebted to Mr Bridgeland for his personal communication on some recent developments.

4 Bion's account first appeared in the 'Lancet' in 1943,
and was subsequently reprinted as the first chapter in
his seminal book, 'Experiences in Groups' (1961).

5 From Tom Main, The Concept of the Therapeutic Community:
Variations and Vicissitudes, given as the first S.H.
Foulkes Annual Lecture in 1977.

6 I am grateful to Pat de Mare for confirming these dates.

7 Foulkes first described these phases in his first book
'Introduction to Group-analytic Psychotherapy' (1948) and
subsequently in his later work, 'Therapeutic Group Analysis' (1964). Quotations are from the earlier work.

8 Main (1977).

9 Maxwell Jones's own accounts of this period can be found
in the introduction to his book 'Social Psychiatry in
Practice' (1968) and in 'The Therapeutic Community, Social
Learning and Social Change' (1979). Quotations are from
Jones (1968).

4 FROM INNOVATION TO APPLICATION

1 This account draws on Jones, 'Social Psychiatry in Practice' (1968) and J.S. Whiteley, The Henderson Hospital
(1980). Quotations are from Jones (1968).

2 E. Barnes (1968).

3 A review of international developments which comments on
their relationship to political attitudes has been written by Clark (1977).

4 Whiteley, Briggs and Turner (1972), part II.

5 Gunn et al. (1978).

6 For an historical account of developments of Tomkins I.
see R. Almond, 'The Healing Community' (1974).

7 See Pullen (1982).

8 For early descriptive accounts of the Phoenix Unit's
development see Mandelbrote (1965) and Sugarman (1968).
My own association with the Phoenix Unit has been a close
one, including an investigation of the way patients' perceptions of themselves change during their stay (Kennard
et al., 1977; Kennard and Clemmey, 1976).

9 For further detail see McGlashen and Levy (1977).

10 For a detailed description and discussion of the development of the Richmond Fellowship, and comparisons between
it and other therapeutic communities see E. Jansen
(1980).

11   The closure of the Marlborough Day Hospital afforded
     occasion for much reflection on the difficulties experi-
     enced there in the last few years.   See, for example,
     R.D. Hinshelwood (1980).
12   A guide to day-care planning which describes this project
     has been produced by R. Blake and D. Millard (1979).

5   SYNANON AND THE CONCEPT-BASED THERAPEUTIC COMMUNITY

1   My account of the early years of Synanon is based on
    Lewis Yablonsky's 'Synanon: The Tunnel Back' (1965).
    Yablonsky was a sociologist, one of the first 'squares'
    (non-addicts) to be accepted by Synanon, who became its
    ally and defender.   His book is not to be looked to for
    impartiality, but for a lively first-hand account of the
    world according to Dederich.
2   For a detailed account of its development see Barry
    Sugarman's 'Daytop Village - A Therapeutic Community'
    (1974).
3   My access to these concepts, and the particular example
    I quote, is through the Ley Community in Oxford, England,
    which in turn derived them from Phoenix House, New York.
    The Ley's first Director was a 'graduate' from that com-
    munity.   It is interesting that although the Ley has
    been established in England for ten years, the termin-
    ology remains American - e.g. 'roller coaster' (English
    - 'big dipper').   This is not untypical.   At inter-
    national meetings staff from many different countries all
    use the same phraseology.
4   A detailed account of Synanon's antecedents is provided
    by F. Glaser (1977).
5   This point is amplified in a useful paper by Paul Antze
    (1979).

6   ALTERNATIVE ASYLUM AND ANTI-PSYCHIATRY

1   For a detailed history see W. Parry-Jones (1981).
2   A brief introduction to Steiner's ideas has been written
    by Watts (1979).
3   A detailed study of successful self-help movements has
    been written by Lieberman, Borman and Associates (1979).
4   'Critical Psychiatry', David Ingleby (ed.) (1981) pro-
    vides an accessible introduction to the work of these two
    men, and some account of recent developments in the ideas
    of anti-psychiatrists.
5   Laing (1971), 'The Politics of the Family and Other
    Essays', p. 58.

6   The anti-psychiatrists were not the first to advocate this
    view.   Donald Winnicott, the famous British psychoanalyst
    and paediatrician, had earlier made the same suggestion.
    Joseph Berke (1979) discusses this point in his book,
    'I Haven't Had to Go Mad Here', p. 125.
7   Much of this evidence is anecdotal - e.g. the various case
    studies described in Berke (1979).   Two more systematic
    investigations of the treatment of acute schizophrenic
    breakdown in therapeutic communities without the use of
    drugs are Mosher et al. (1975) and McGlashan and Levy
    (1977).
8   Cooper's account of this experiment at Shenley Hospital's
    Villa 21, where he worked from 1962 to 1966, is contained
    in his 'Psychiatry and Anti-Psychiatry' (1967).
9   These figures are taken from Laing (1971) and Berke
    (1980).
10 Berke (1980).
11 M. Schatzman (1969).
12 Raymond Blake, personal communication.
13 Barnes and Berke (1971).
14 See Berke (1979), Chapters 5 and 6.
15 Mosher et al. (1975).

PART II

1   Barnes and Berke (1971), Mahony (1979).
      Mahony's account vividly conveys the interaction
    between a resident's private thoughts and feelings and
    the impact of the values and relationships within the
    community.   The process by which a therapeutic commu-
    nity can gradually redirect delinquents' energies into
    socially constructive channels is movingly illuminated.
    However not all residents respond positively - see for
    example Mike Smith's account of his stay in two other
    therapeutic communities (Smith, 1971).   See also 'The
    Consumer's Perspective' in Jansen (1980).

10 QUESTIONS OF TRAINING

1   Caine, Wijesinghe and Winter (1981), Chapters 1, 2 and 4.
2   More details of this follow-up study are reported in
    Kennard and Roberts (1980).

References

Ahlin, G. (1981), A Model for Institutional Development Towards Therapeutic Community, 'Group Analysis', 14, pp. 57-63.

Almond, R. (1974), 'The Healing Community', New York, Jason Aronson.

Antze, P. (1979), The Role of Ideologies in Peer Psychotherapy Groups in M. Lieberman and L.D. Borman, 'Self-help Groups for Coping with Crisis', London, Jossey-Bass.

Barnes, E. (1968) (ed.), 'Psychosocial Nursing: Studies from the Cassel Hospital', London, Tavistock.

Barnes, M. and Berke, J. (1971), 'Mary Barnes: Two Accounts of a Journey Through Madness', London, Hart-Davis Mac-Gibbon.

Berke, J. (1979), 'I Haven't Had to Go Mad Here', Harmondsworth, Penguin.

Berke, J. (1980), Kingsley Hall in 'The Therapeutic Community', E. Jansen (ed.), London, Croom Helm.

Bessin, A. (1977), The Miracle of the Therapeutic Community: from Birth to Post-partum Insanity to Full Recovery in 'Proceedings of the 2nd World Conference of Therapeutic Communities', Montreal, Portage Press.

Bion, W.R. (1961), 'Experiences in Groups', London, Tavistock.

Blake, R. and Millard, D. (1979), 'The Therapeutic Community in Day Care', London, Association of Therapeutic Communities.

Bockoven, J.S. (1956), Moral Treatment in American Society, 'Journal of Nervous and Mental Diseases', 124, pp. 167-94.

Bridgeland, M. (1971), 'Pioneer Work with Maladjusted Children', London, Staples Press.

Brown, D. and Pedder, J. (1978), 'Introduction to Psychotherapy', London, Social Science Paperbacks.

Caine, T.M.,Wijesinghe, O.B.A. and Winter, D.A. (1981), 'Personal Styles in Neurosis', London, Routledge & Kegan Paul.

Caudill, W.A. (1958), 'The Psychiatric Hospital as a small Society', Cambridge, Mass., Harvard University Press.

Clark, D.H. (1964), 'Administrative Therapy', London, Tavistock.

Clark, D.H. (1965), The Therapeutic Community - concept, practice and future, 'British Journal of Psychiatry', 111, pp. 947-54.

Clark, D.H. (1977), Therapeutic Community, 'British Journal of Psychiatry', 131, pp. 553-64.

Cooper, D. (1967), 'Psychiatry and Anti-Psychiatry', London, Tavistock.

Foulkes, S.H. (1948), 'Introduction to Group-analytic Psychiatry', London, Heinemann.

Foulkes, S.H. (1964), 'Therapeutic Group Analysis', London, George Allen & Unwin.

Frank, J. (1979), What is Psychotherapy? in S. Block (ed.), 'An Introduction to the Psychotherapies', Oxford University Press.

Freeman, H. (ed.) (1965), 'Psychiatric Hospital Care', London, Baillere, Tindall & Cassell.

Glaser, F. (1977), The Origins of the Drug-free Therapeutic Community - a Retrospective History, 'Proceedings of the 2nd World Conference of Therapeutic Communities', P. Vamos and J.E. Brown (eds), Montreal, Portage Press.

Goffman, E. (1961), 'Aylums', New York, Doubleday, republished (1968), Harmondsworth, Penguin.

Gunn, J. et al. (1978), 'Psychiatric Aspects of Imprisonment', London, Academic Press.

Hinshelwood, R.D. (1980), The seeds of disaster, 'International Journal of Therapeutic Communities', 1 (3) pp. 181-8.

Hobson, R.F. (1979), The Messianic Community in 'Therapeutic Communities - Reflections and Progress', R.D. Hinshelwood and N. Mannings(eds), London, Routledge & Kegan Paul.

Illich, I. et al. (1977), 'Disabling Professions', London, Marion Boyers.

Ingleby, D. (ed.) (1981), 'Critical Psychiatry', Harmondsworth, Penguin.

Jansen, E. (1980) (ed.), 'The Therapeutic Community', London, Croom Helm.

Jones, M. (1968), 'Social Psychiatry in Practice', Harmondsworth, Penguin.

Jones, M. (1979), The Therapeutic Community, Social Learning and Social Change in R.D. Hinshelwood and N. Manning (eds), 'Therapeutic Community - Reflections and Progress', London, Routledge & Kegan Paul.

Kennard, D. and Clemmey, R. (1976), Psychiatric patients as seen by self and others: an exploration of change in a

Therapeutic Community setting, 'British Journal of Medical Psychology', 49, pp. 35-53.

Kennard, D., Clemmey, R. and Mandelbrote, B. (1977), Aspects of Outcome in a Therapeutic Community Setting, 'British Journal of Psychiatry', 130, pp. 475-80.

Kennard, D. and Roberts, J. (1980), Therapeutic Community Training - a one year follow up, 'Group Analysis', 13 (1), pp. 54-6.

Kreeger, L. (1975) (ed.), 'The Large Group', London, Constable.

Laing, R.D. (1967), 'The Politics of Experience', Harmondsworth, Penguin.

Laing, R.D. (1971), 'The Politics of the Family and Other Essays', London, Tavistock.

Lieberman, M., Borman, L. and Associates (1979), 'Self-help Groups for Coping with Crisis', London, Jossey-Bass.

McGlashen, T.H. and Levy, S.T. (1977), Sealing-over in a Therapeutic Community, 'Psychiatry', 40, pp. 55-65.

Mahony, N. (1979), My Stay at the Henderson Therapeutic Community in R.D. Hinshelwood and N. Manning, 'Therapeutic Communities: Reflections and Progress', London, Routledge & Kegan Paul.

Main, T. (1946), The Hospital as a Therapeutic Institution, 'Bulletin of the Mennings Clinic', 10, pp. 66-70.

Main, T. (1975), Some Psychodynamics of large groups in 'The Large Group', (ed.) L. Kreeger, London, Constable.

Main, T. (1977), The Concept of the Therapeutic Community: Variations and Vicissitudes, lecture given as first S.H. Foulkes annual lecture, subsequently reprinted as a supplement to 'Group Analysis', 10 (2) (1977).

Maller, J.O. (1971), 'The Therapeutic Community with Chronic Mental Patients', London, S. Karger.

Mandelbrote, B.M. (1965), The Use of Psychodynamic and Sociodynamic Principles in the Treatment of Psychotics, 'Comprehensive Psychiatry', 6 (6) pp. 381-7.

Martin, D. (1962), 'Adventure in Psychiatry', London, Cassirer.

Moos, R. (1974), 'Evaluating Treatment Environments: A Social Ecological Approach', New York, Wiley.

Moreno, J.L. (1977), 'Psychodrama', 5th edn, New York, Beacon House.

Mosher, L.R. et al. (1975), Soteria: Evaluation of a home-based treatment for schizophrenia, 'American Journal of Orthopsychiatry', 45, pp. 455-67.

Parry-Jones, W. (1981), The Model of the Geel Lunatic colony and its influence on the nineteenth century asylum system in Britain in A. Scull (ed.), 'Madness, Mad Doctors and Madmen', London, Athlene Press.

Price, R.H. and Moos, R. (1975), Towards a Taxonomy of in-patient treatment Environments, 'Journal of Abnormal Psychology', 84, pp. 181-8.

Pullen, G. (1982), Street - the 17 day Community, 'International Journal of Therapeutic Communities', 2 (2).

Rapoport, R.N. (1960), 'Community as Doctor', London, Tavistock.

Rothman, D. (1971), 'The Discovery of the Asylum', Boston, Little, Brown.

Schatzman, M. (1969), Madness and Morals, in 'Counter - Culture', J. Berke (ed.), London, Peter Owen.   Reprinted in 'Laing and Anti-Psychiatry' (eds) Boyers & Orrill (1972), Harmondsworth, Penguin.

Schoenberg, E. (1972), 'A Hospital Looks at Itself', London, Cassirer.

Scull, A. (1979), 'Museums of Madness', London, Allen Lane.

Smith, M. (1981), Working my ticket, 'International Journal of Therapeutic Communities', 2 (1), pp. 43-51.

Stanton, A. and Schwartz, M. (1954), 'The Mental Hospital', Basic Books.

Storr, A. (1979), 'The Art of Psychotherapy', London, Secker & Warburg/Heinemann.

Sugarman, B. (1968), The Phoenix Unit, Alliance against illness, 'New Society', London, New Science Publications.

Sugarman, B. (1974), 'Daytop Village - A Therapeutic Community', New York, Holt, Rinehart & Winston.

Watts, F. (1979), The Objective Imagination: Rudolf Steiner and Clinical Psychology, 'New Forum', 6 (2), pp. 31-3.

Whiteley, J.S. (1980), The Henderson Hospital, 'International Journal of Therapeutic Communities', 1 (1), pp. 38-58.

Whiteley, J.S., Briggs, D. and Turner, M. (1972), 'Dealing with Deviants', London, Hogarth Press.

Yablonsky, L. (1965), 'Synanon: The Tunnel Back', New York, Macmillan.

Index